HOW TO MEET, THINK, AND WORK TO CONSENSUS

HOW TO MEET, THINK, AND WORK TO CONSENSUS

Daniel A. Tagliere

Pfeiffer
& COMPANY

Amsterdam • Johannesburg • London
San Diego • Sydney • Toronto

Pfeiffer & Company
8517 Production Avenue
San Diego, CA 92121-2280 USA
(619) 578-5900 Fax (619) 578-2042

This publication is designed to provide accurate and authoritative information in regard to the subject matter covered. It is sold with the understanding that the publisher is not engaged in rendering legal, accounting, or other professional service. If legal advice or other expert assistance is required, the services of a competent professional person should be sought. *From a Declaration of Principles jointly adopted by a Committee of the American Bar Association and a Committee of Publishers.*

Editor: JoAnn Padgett
Interior Designer: Susan Odelson
Cover: John Odam Design Associates

ISBN:
Trade Paper 0-89384-225-7
Hardcover 0-88390-339-3

Library of Congress Cataloging-in-Publication Data

Tagliere, Daniel A.
How to meet, think, and work to consensus/Daniel Tagliere
    p. cm.
ISBN 0-88390-339-3
1. Work groups. 2. Meetings. 3. Small groups.
4. Group problem solving. 5. Decision-making, Group
I. Title.

HD66.T34   1992   92-28629
658.4'036—dc20   CIP

Printed in the United States of America.
Printing 1 2 3 4 5 6 7 8 9 10

DEDICATION

To the prophet who said it first and who said it best.

"Come now, let us reason together."
Isaiah 1:17-18

CONTENTS

ACKNOWLEDGMENTS

I am indebted to the many teams who helped me learn by permitting me to facilitate them, and to my direct and indirect colleagues and teammates who have generously contributed their ideas. I specifically wish to acknowledge Laura Jo Tagliere, Walter Hamester, and Richard Bartels for their ideas and help with the manuscript.

1

INTRODUCTION

Never doubt that a small group of thoughtful,
committed citizens can change the world; indeed,
it is the only thing that ever has.
Margaret Mead

This book presents a process for improving small group meetings, which are so important in work organizations but so often ineffective and frustrating to participants. Our goal is to give you a process that you can use time and time again to find your own solution to difficult situations. This book describes the steps of that process. The initial step is to create a plan for team members detailing who, what, where, when, why, and how. Once a plan is in place, the next step is to select the team members needed to complete the project. With a team in place, ground rules are established. Then a system for getting things done is devised along with a method for controlling and recording events. We offer multiple options for idea generation and decision making. The book's many options and effective techniques are meant to be used creatively by you.

Others have labeled consensual processes similar to the ones presented in this book as "Collaborative Thinking," "Group Problem Solving," or "Consensus Decision Making." To differentiate systematic thinking from the relatively undisciplined but more common variety of thinking, I use "Teamwork Thinking" for the process and "Think Team" for those engaged in it. The process must not be confused with group think, which is a pejorative term that describes the various phenomena that tend to defeat rational thinking and objective decision making in meetings.

I define "Teamwork Thinking" as two or more people meeting, thinking, and working together in a highly organized and systematic manner to review information, generate ideas, and make decisions in order to change some present situation to some desired situation. This broad definition is meant to encompass all systematic and collaborative small group activities serving such purposes as creative, scientific, and detective problem solving; strategic, organizational, marketing, and project planning; quality or productivity improvement; and negotiating and other organizational transformation efforts. I often use the term "problem solving" collectively to cover all of these activities.

We all intuitively solve problems every day of our lives; we seldom solve them in a conscious, systematic manner and, very rarely, with others. So if, in spite of any negative group meeting experiences you may have had, you still appreciate the potential power of systematic team thinking and want to develop a team or participate more effectively as a team member, then this book is for you.

Group meetings are often the scene of win/lose situations. Consider typical events that occur in group meetings—people don't listen because they are thinking of what they want to say, members interrupt each other, ideas or suggestions are made but not acknowledged, and people choose sides to support one idea against another. Instead of collaborating together to realize their goal or to make the best decision, the group members act like competing individuals. One way to adjust this kind of situation is to try to make decisions by consensus instead of by democratic or majority rule.

To solve problems in a collaborative and creative way, it is necessary to adopt a cultural norm for dealing with all win/lose situations. For example:

1. View all win/lose situations as problems that can be solved in a positive manner.
2. Involve all stakeholders or their representatives.
3. Insist that they be consensus seekers.
4. Utilize an acceptable and appropriate process.

Currently, the most common methods to effect change are to fight or to negotiate. When people have something and they want something else, it frequently and increasingly seems to be only obtainable at the expense of others who already have what they want or want something that is obstructive to what others want. Win/lose situations should not be seen as zero/sum conflicts where someone has to lose and someone has to win. Instead they should be seen as situations where Teamwork Thinking must be applied to achieve a win/win situation.

Stakeholders in a problem situation are those who have a vital interest in the problem and any change that a solution may cause. Involving others in the problem-solving process has two main advantages: more brain power is brought to bear on the problem and more support is generated for whatever solution is found. The more immediately the problem impacts others, the more important it is that others participate in solving the problem. Otherwise the solved problem may give rise to another, more serious problem.

Consensus seekers understand that the only way to truly win, to get what they want and to keep it, is to make sure all parties involved also get what they want. To make the approach work, all parties have to recognize this practicality and be genuinely concerned that all parties' needs are met, though never at the expense of another.

After the group recognizes that it wants to change something and adopt the win/win philosophy, it must use an effective process. The Teamwork-Thinking process, or some variation of it, is now being used in a relatively small number of work organizations. Strategic, organizational, marketing, and project planning or some variety of problem solving, quality improvement, or productivity enhancement are the more common activities to which Teamwork Thinking is applied.

The concepts, tools, and techniques offered in this book have been evolving through many years of work with client teams and through collaboration in the design and development of seminars, training materials, and computer software for Teamwork Thinking. We have helped many teams in many different organizations with great success.

Even untrained teams are usually better than individuals at solving problems, but this result is not the common perception. Most people have had a number of negative experiences attempting to make decisions in groups. Such negative results should be expected if the individuals involved have different viewpoints, backgrounds, skills, and capacities and if the group is dealing with complex issues with emotional overtones. This kind of experience makes many doubt the power of Teamwork Thinking.

It usually is not very difficult to prove that "two heads are better than one." Almost everyone buys into that saying once you specify that the brains in the heads are equal in capacity, experiences, skill, and motivation.

Respect for every team member's views and the seeking of full consensus for decisions by the team are key tenants of the process. Consensus seeking, which is used here to mean complete agreement of all group members, promotes a fuller examination of the facts, the generation of more ideas, and more careful decision making. It also tends to make team members feel better about their work together and, therefore, makes them more supportive of the team's decisions.

Teamwork Thinking and similar processes have been slow to catch on due to the nature of most organizations. Most organizations are hierarchically structured. The typical organization chart is a diagram of power. The single most powerful person is at the top followed by one or more layers of managers and, finally, down to the least powerful at the bottom of the pyramid.

Small group meetings are a microcosm of the organization phenomenon. The most powerful person sits at the head of the table, does most of the talking, and makes the decisions. In other meetings the more powerful figures may not have formal rank as their source of strength, but may obtain their power to dominate because of a number of situational and personal factors. For example, some meetings may be peopled by individuals representing constituencies with no direct power link to others in the room. Power to control is achieved by the size and influence of their constituencies. Personal power is based on perceptions. An individual who is seen as more experienced, intelligent, or wise, or who represents a subgrouping of the human race, will be more powerful. We all carry around in our heads these social rankings depending on the situation and our personal belief and value system. In some cases men may have more status than women, adults more than children, upper social classes more than lower social classes, and so on.

Whether power distinction is formal or whether it has been assumed, it is predictably a corrupter of the Teamwork-Thinking process. What about a person whose power is based on far superior knowledge or skill related to what a team is working on— does that person deserve the power to lead and even make decisions for the team? The answer is an emphatic no! In the first place, few problems for which a team would be assembled are simple enough to trust to one person regardless of his or her expertise. Second, even a very wise person can learn or be stimulated by those less knowledgeable, and it is the synergism of the collective mental gifts, information, and meeting skills that makes the team superior to any individual. Therefore rank and power must be ignored if the team really wishes to get the best possible information, ideas, and decisions. Power is difficult to ignore, even in meetings governed by consensus rules, but it can and is being done in organizations with leaders who support Teamwork Thinking.

Just as the real work of the White House is not done by the president and the work of Congress is done in subcommittees and not in full sessions, really important thinking and decision making should be done in small groups.

Over time we have developed the art and skill of educating individual minds. We now also know how to organize, train, and empower groups of problem solvers, or Think Teams. Just as some computational tasks need networks of individual computers to co-process the work to be done, we all need to learn how to team up to fulfill our human destiny.

Even though a leader can rarely be as effective when planning and problem solving as the right team, I am not suggesting that we can do without leaders and individual problem solvers and decision makers. Vision, initiative, and risk taking must not be suppressed under the banner of consensus seeking. Team Thinking can and should be used to blend individual and collective wisdom. Time and the other pressures prevalent in the typical work organization require that most day-to-day problem solving and decision making be done without calling a meeting. Many great undertakings are almost solely the result of one person's vision, dedication, and efforts. Great leaders pursue new visions, encourage individual initiative, and value their ability to meet, think, and work participatively with the best minds available.

If you want to be a great team leader, start by learning about Teamwork Thinking. Although I have been training and facilitating teams in a great variety of organizations for many years, I am constantly awed by the power and potential teams display when properly prepared. I believe you will be as well, if you apply the tools and techniques offered in this book to your team's work.

2

SELECT, BOND, AND EMPOWER TEAMMATES

A group becomes a team when each member is sure enough of himself and his contribution to praise the skills of the others.
Norman Shidle

The purpose of this chapter is to help you become more adept at selecting the best available candidates for Think Teams and to forge a stronger commitment among all team members to the team's mission, assignments, and decisions. This goal is accomplished by helping members to become more aware of how they think, feel, and behave in meetings and to understand why they do so.

Team Member Selection

It is important that those you invite to become members of a Think Team have the opportunity to decline the invitation. Only those who want to serve can serve well. Although there may be degrees of interest among those invited, none should attend who are absolutely uninterested even if you have the authority to order them to attend. If you have a choice, keep the numbers down. Five to seven participants seems to be ideal. Fewer members means more time for each member to contribute.

As the team's organizer, you will have a general idea of what the team will work on. It may be a single-purpose team or one that will deal with a whole family of issues. The team may be a manager and those who report to him or her, or any other group of people. Criteria to consider as you select your teammates include knowledge, wisdom, and astuteness. Ask how much the candidate knows about what the team will be working on. Pooling ignorance, even in a very systematic way, is not likely to yield significant results.

Other things to consider include

1. *Practical Experience:* What is the candidate's background in the area the team will focus on?

2. *Technical Skills:* What abilities does the candidate have that the team may find useful?

3. *Freedom:* To what extent is the candidate free to work with and for the team, rather than for some outside person, cause, or organization?

4. *Resources:* What time, tools, personnel, money, and supplies can the candidate contribute to the team's efforts?

5. *Status:* To what extent will the candidate's power, prestige, reputation, and influence contribute to the team's efforts?

6. *Objectivity:* Is the candidate free from excessive emotional baggage that may hinder the team's work?

7. *Style:* Is the candidate's style—how she or he thinks, communicates, and interacts—one that will work successfully with other team members?

8. *Availability:* Does the candidate have time to attend team meetings and to perform assigned tasks?

9. *Team Skills:* Does the candidate know how to function in team meetings or, at least, appear to be able to learn quickly?

10. *Concern/Interest:* Is the general area of team focus one that is important to the candidate?

11. *Cost of Participation:* How much will the person, the team, or the organization have to spend in money and time? Can the organization or the team afford the candidate's time taken from other duties?

Team Member Bonding

Usually new teams need time for the members to get acquainted. Existing teams may need to change the relationship patterns established by precedent and preconceptions before real work begins. It helps to know, like, respect, and feel comfortable with the other members of a Think Team. This familiarity can come with experience, but the process can be accelerated by helping the members become aware of personality characteristics that are particularly important to Teamwork Thinking: communication style, decision-making style, values, and self-concept. This assumes that all members are otherwise qualified by ability, experience, and motivation. Ideally, the dominant feeling should be one of mutual respect and confidence among teammates, but members should also have the personal confidence and the inner strength that permits honest disagreement to surface and be examined. All of this comes from achieving a certain level of mental intimacy among team members.

Styles, values, and self-concept are not factors to be considered good or bad, but they should not be ignored. They are real and do affect the performance of the team. It helps to be aware of these factors and to make allowances for them during team meetings.

Communication Style

Communication style combines the extent to which a person tries to help others understand the messages he or she is sending and how much that person tries to understand others when receiving their messages. Some people subconsciously change their communication style depending on the situation, but most do not. It is possible to learn how to consciously send and receive more effectively if the learner knows how he or she is being perceived by others.

This can be accomplished by having each member ask the others how they perceive him or her as a receiver and sender of information and if these perceptions influence their interactions. As the Scottish poet Robert Burns said, "O God that gift, thy giftie gie us to see ourselves as other see us." Most people aren't very aware of how they come across to others. They can become more effective in team meetings if they make the attempt to be perceived as communicating well. The importance of being perceived as an objective yet collaborative team player is as important as effectively sharing information and ideas.

Decision-Making Style

Decision-making or thinking style refers primarily to how a person tends to make up his or her mind when a decision is called for. Some make quick, intuitive decisions; others slow and analytical ones, and still others switch from one to the other with relative ease, depending on the decision being made. Either style may be good or bad depending on the situation. Creative, intuitive people can sometimes quickly grasp a complex situation and come up with just the right idea. On the other hand, they may be impatient with situations requiring careful, perhaps tedious examination of minute detail. Details are of tremendous importance in some decisions and overlooking them can have grave consequences. Analytical people have the capacity for deliberately examining all elements and viewpoints, but they may spend more time and energy than the issue warrants. This delay can sometimes irritate others who may settle for a quicker, even if less perfect, decision. By focusing on detail, analytical people sometimes fail to grasp the big picture.

Patience and acceptance are the key words for dealing with those people whose decision-making style is significantly different from yours. You may have to wait as a teammate ponders an issue. That slow thinker may see something you don't, and that fast thinker may have just cut through to the heart of the issue and saved the rest of the team a lot of tedious work. It helps to have a variety of styles on the team because different phases of the problem-solving process call for different approaches.

Styles are tendencies toward behaving in a certain way, not ironclad patterns. People can consciously modify their styles to fit the need of the moment. For example, when the decision is of extreme importance to a person, such as buying a home, he or she becomes more analytical than when making a minor purchase such as a new book. It would be ideal if every member were aware of his or her own style and those of his or her teammates and took this information into consideration when solving problems or planning. Having team members talk about their own styles and their perceptions of the styles of others is a simple, yet effective way of getting better acquainted.

Values

Values refer to the relative importance that people place on ideas, beliefs, and actions. On the loftier end, we might call these values "morals." We believe some things to be good and, therefore, to be adhered to regardless of how impractical they might be in a given situation. In other cases, values can rightfully be called "preferences." This is the case when you can simply like one thing better than another. Those things we value more will take preference over those we value less and, therefore, affect our perceptions, thoughts, feelings, decisions, and actions. It helps to know the values of your teammates because such knowledge will enable you to understand and deal with them more effectively. For example, if a person has a high disregard for money, it would be foolish to try to convince him or her to make a certain decision based on the profit that would result from the decision.

You can start a lively discussion among teammates and help them to learn about their values by discussing the relative importance of an organization's stakeholder groups. Stakeholders are those who have a vital interest in an organization and who also can influence an organization's success. The relative importance of these groups depends on the viewpoint of the person(s) asked. The five stakeholder groups are

1. The owners or controllers (top management) of the organization;
2. The clients or customers (those served by the organization);
3. The members (those who do the work of the organization);
4. Society (the community, government, citizens in general); and
5. The suppliers (those who fulfill the organization's requirements for equipment, information, and supplies).

How people weight the importance of the various stakeholders will influence the decisions they make. In a typical organization, financial people tend to be concerned with the owner's interest in earning an acceptable return on his or her investment. Human resources people tend to favor the employees; salespeople favor the clients; and the purchasing department will at least be somewhat sympathetic to the suppliers.

A person's value system can inhibit objectivity. How he or she feels influences perceptions, such as the devoted mother who sees her son as a "good boy" even though a judge and jury see him as a criminal. Subconsciously, nearly everyone seeks evidence to support his or her own belief system and overlooks those facts that argue against it. While this very human characteristic will never be eliminated in team meetings, it helps if people are aware of their own and their teammates' values that are pertinent to the work of the team. Openly discussing values tends to foster objectivity about the team's work.

Self-Concept

A person's self-concept is the sense of who he or she is, where he or she came from, and where he or she is going. While team members may not have consciously thought about these things, they do have a "working" answer to all of them, and these answers do influence how they live their lives and how they work with others in team situations. It is difficult to really understand a teammate without knowing his or her self-concept. Therefore, encourage teammates to respectfully listen to each other as they tell about their families, education, career, turning points in their lives, the things that are currently most pressing on their minds, their goals and ambitions, and the things that they hope they will be remembered for when they are gone.

The turning points or key events that change lives are typically getting married, having children, discovering a latent talent, or achieving a certain new status. These are clues as to how a person sees his or her destiny and, therefore, clues as to what will motivate future behavior. A person's current "hot buttons" are those concerns that are high on his or her personal agenda. It could be an actual or pending family tragedy or something as mildly distracting as a golf game planned for next week. If the emotions connected with the event are strong, it will influence how the person works on the team's assignments.

The future, or what a person is looking forward to, is a clue as to how he or she will devote energy to the team's assignments. What a person would like to be remembered for after he or she has gone can also be shared to mutual advantage. Most people never get an opportunity to tell others about their self-concept, and most everybody would like others to know they have one. Everyone wants to be recognized as a real person with interests and concerns outside of the group, even if they never expect the team to specifically use the information. The entire process of learning about teammates breeds a certain respectful intimacy that smooths interpersonal processes even when the team is focused on the most technical of issues. The team, then, becomes a group of bonded friends that feels more confident about who they are and what they can contribute.

Team Empowerment

Empowerment means giving a team the authority necessary to achieve its mission or primary purpose. There are basically only two types of Think Teams: those that can make decisions and implement them and those that are limited to making recommendations to others who have the power to approve and implement the decisions. In the latter case, where team members are accountable to other individuals or constituencies, the nature of the empowerment must be made clear. If it is not, the team's motivation, morale, and effectiveness will be mitigated. It is important that the nature and extent of empowerment be fully discussed and accepted during the team bonding process.

Developing a bond between members based on mutual understanding and acceptance of individual communication and decision-making styles, values, and self-concepts is very important. However, it is not as important to the bonding process as winning. Winning means that the team experiences success in working together, in getting something accomplished that it knows it could not have done better or could not have achieved through any other method. Success breeds success. This saying is as true for teams as it is for individuals.

3

SHARE INFORMATION THROUGH CLEAR COMMUNICATION

Everything that can be thought at all can be thought clearly.
Everything that can be said can be said clearly.
Ludwig Wittgenstein

I t is important to recognize that the products of a Think
Team in meetings are the facts and ideas offered by team
members and the decisions the team makes. These should
be recorded on flip chart pages or on an overhead projector
so that all members can see every word that is being
recorded. The sharing of information and ideas in Think
Team meetings is disciplined, for the most part, by the
work procedure the team elects to follow. The "Work
Procedure," which is more fully explained in Chapter
Seven, is a logical series of steps that is presented through
questions. The team's work becomes that of listing an-
swers/statements in response to each question. Therefore,
the sharing of information is much different than is usually
found in everyday discussions and traditional meetings.

The primary method of sharing information in meetings is the interactive process of personal communication
that includes listening, speaking, nonverbal communications, and feedback. This chapter will help you become
more aware of interpersonal communication processes and
how you can use them to make your Think Team meetings
more productive.

Listening

Listening is an underused skill because of the common
misconception that leaders generally give orders and followers listen. Therefore, those who wish to exert their
authority or dominance tend to talk more than listen. When
engaged in Teamwork Thinking, all members must treat

listening as an extremely important function and not as a subordinate function or as an interruption of your contributions to the team's activities.

Effective listening starts with letting the speaker know you are ready and willing to listen. Indicate your full attention by looking at the speaker and by being patient while he or she speaks. The two techniques that will help you listen for information more effectively are distinguishing fact from opinion and support checking.

Fact or Opinion

Facts are statements that can be proven to be true to an objective observer through demonstration or logic. While few things can be proven to be absolutely true in the philosophical sense, everyday "working" facts can be identified by the careful listener who is aware of his or her own frame of reference and that of the person speaking. Don't be misled by irrelevant facts; true statements may have no bearing on the issue at hand. Ask people "why" questions when they offer facts and opinions that don't seem particularly true or relevant rather than challenging them directly. "Why do you think this fact is true and pertinent to our discussion?" This will help them rethink and restate their views and enhance understanding.

Facts can then be logically manipulated to deduce new facts. Frequently we confuse opinions and assumptions with facts. In some cases we do not have hard facts to deal with and must resort to using assumptions, probable facts, or even loosely held opinions or guesses. Recognize that few things can be proven to be absolutely true and take as facts those statements that can be proven to be true to the team's satisfaction.

Here are some guidelines for grading facts. They are listed in rank order from most effective to least effective.

1. Facts that can be proven repeatedly to be true to the satisfaction of reasonable, knowledgeable, and critical people;

2. Facts based on your own firsthand observations;

3. Secondhand facts—those attested to as true by a trusted, firsthand observer;

4. Facts that can be logically inferred from either repeatedly provable or firsthand facts;

5. Facts inferred from secondhand facts or a combination of first- and secondhand facts;

6. Strongly held opinions by respected or authoritative resource persons; and

7. Statements that reflect misperceptions, misconceptions, wrong assumptions, faulty logic, and the prejudices of the person offering the opinion as fact.

Opinions are statements that may be true or merely guesses based on misinterpretations of facts that reflect the viewpoint of the speaker but can't be proven: for example, "The bridge is going to collapse." The degree of confidence a person has in an opinion may convince him or her it is a fact and may influence others to believe it as well. Some opinions can be considered more valuable than others based on the speaker's reputation with the listener.

Support Checking

Support checking is the process of listening with the intent of identifying the main points the speaker is presenting and the facts, opinions, examples, and other things he or she might say to support the main points. This enables you to sort out the information you receive and to estimate the validity of the facts being presented. In the following paragraph, try to identify the main point and the supporting statements for it. Then, judge the degree of validity of each supporting statement and the extent to which it supports the main point.

> The bridge is going to collapse. It trembles when a small truck is driven over it. It is over a hundred years old. No maintenance has been performed on it for the past five years. We've had heavy rains for weeks now, and the girders are deteriorated. I don't like the looks of it at all. I've looked at bridges all my life and, while I'm no structural engineer, I see a disaster in the making. Everyone around here is just waiting for the crash. We ought to tear it down.

Obviously, the speaker's main point is that the bridge is going to collapse so it should be torn down. Many of the statements support this contention but vary considerably in validity and relevance. This position could be carefully analyzed and rated to get at the probable truth, but in the course of general discussion, the individual listener must develop an almost intuitive sense about the logic of the speaker's statements and then probe to determine if the speaker's contention is to be accepted.

Speaking

Speaking starts with getting your listener's attention and permission to talk. These two preliminary steps signal that an important message is coming and prepare the listener to receive it. If the discussion is confused and undisciplined, don't hesitate to ask for attention directly with a question such as, "May I have your full attention? I have some important information to give you."

There are several key speaking qualities that will help you communicate more effectively in team meetings: logical structure, clarity, and congruent nonverbal messages.

Logical Structure

There are several useful formats or procedures to follow when speaking, but the time honored "Tell what you are going to tell, tell it, and then tell what you have told" is usually more than adequate for most Think Team meetings. To tell everything that your listener needs to know, you can use who, what, why, where, when, and how as a guide.

It is also helpful to number your points when explaining something. For example, "I have three things I want to tell you. First, the project is over budget; second, our deadlines will have to be adjusted; third, our responsibilities have been expanded." You should give your listener supporting statements for those points that need further explanation or proof. Try to use facts for your supporting statements and to identify the source of your facts. When you use opinions, acknowledge as much.

Clarity

Speak in complete sentences. Don't assume, even among close acquaintances, that people will understand phrases and verbal signals that are abundantly clear to you. The complete sentence rule also holds true when writing on flip chart pages. A bullet or dash and an abbreviation or phrase will not only mean different things to different teammates but also may lose all meaning as time progresses and the original concept becomes obscured.

Use clear, unambiguous terms. Avoid slang, vulgar language, and jargon. Use relatively short sentences and say only what is necessary to get your point across. Avoid abstract terms and concepts as much as possible. Choose descriptive words and phrases appropriate to your message. When you want to make sure you are understood, simply ask your teammates what they have heard you say before they react to your message. This permits you to make corrections before the discussion takes off in other directions.

Congruent Nonverbal Communication

Nonverbal communication or body language, as it is frequently called, refers to facial expressions, posture, hand gestures, and movements. To be congruent, your body language must match your verbal message. People will often judge the importance of your remarks more by your tone of voice, demeanor, and actions than by the meaning of your words.

There are no hard and fast rules for interpreting body language signals when listening or observing others because personal habits, cultural traditions, and special circumstances all influence them. You can, however, make some general assumptions based on your own experiences and by getting to know your teammates. If you want to give a body language message that says you are seriously intent upon communicating, look the person in the eye without glaring, keep your body alert but relaxed, and avoid doing anything else like writing, reading, or moving about.

Feedback

There are two types of feedback used in interpersonal communications: Feeling Feedback and Factual Feedback. Both are used to help the party receiving the feedback to judge how well he or she is being understood by the other party and, thereby, be in a position to confirm understanding or correct misunderstanding.

Factual Feedback

Factual Feedback is the process of making sure you understand the content of what the speaker is saying or making sure your listener understands the content of your message. Content refers to factual information as opposed to emotional information. Factual Feedback can be given in several ways. The methods listed below are in rank order from most effective to least effective.

1. Taking some action that proves you understand.
2. Asking questions that imply understanding.
3. Giving examples that prove you understand.
4. Interpreting and restating what you heard the speaker say and giving him or her the opportunity to correct you if necessary.
5. Repeating what the speaker has said.
6. Showing by your facial expression, body language, or through nonverbal sounds that you do or don't understand the speaker.

Factual Feedback should be a part of every communication exchange if you want to be sure understanding has taken place. Most often the failure to seek or to offer feedback creates or compounds what we usually call "communication problems." Both the speaker and listener have the obligation to communicate effectively, and feedback is the most reliable method for doing so.

Feeling Feedback

Feeling Feedback is the process of empathizing or letting other people know you understand how they feel. This process helps factual communication take place because people exchange factual information and think more clearly when their emotional state is acknowledged.

Emotions can be described as being basically positive or negative depending on whether the person experiencing the emotion feels good or bad. Positive emotions would include joy, delight, happiness, and contentment. Negative emotions would include anger, hostility, and disgust. It is quite common to have mixed emotions; for example, a political candidate might feel sad to lose but glad not to have to make another campaign speech.

You can let other people know your emotional state by simply telling them how you feel during the course of the conversation. "I'm really worried about this job being done right. On the other hand, I'm glad you're working with me on the project." Articulating your emotional state helps you to sort out your feelings and keep them in check so you can deal with the issue objectively.

People feel understood and comfortable when they sense you know how they feel and that you seem to care. You can help another person to communicate more effectively by relating how you think he or she is feeling so that the individual can acknowledge his or her feelings personally as well as to you.

Avoid judgmental statements like, "You're being immature about this issue." Instead, state what you believe to be the case, why, and how it makes you feel. Take responsibility for the statements you make by using "I" whenever practical. For example, "I get the impression that you're feeling good about this project because of the way you're smiling and practically dancing around, and I want you to know it makes me happy as well."

Try to give a lot more positive Feeling Feedback messages than negative ones. Positive messages build a much stronger foundation for the relationship and enable the other person to accept your negative feedback messages in the spirit in which they are intended. This concept and technique is covered more fully in the next chapter.

Communication Skills Assessment

As a team development activity, every team member could ask every other member to evaluate his or her communication skills. This would enable every team member to know where to concentrate individual improvement efforts. Simply ask members to grade everyone else from 1 (low) to 5 (high) for each of the areas listed below and, if possible, to cite actual examples to support their grades.

1. Structure: How well do I organize my messages?
2. Clarity: How clear do I usually make myself?
3. Conciseness: Do I keep my messages both accurate and brief?
4. Completeness: Do I give all of the information that I should?
5. Concreteness: How well do I stick to the facts?
6. Congruency: Does my body language match my words?
7. Factual Feedback: How well do I ensure that accurate communication has taken place?
8. Feeling Feedback: How effectively do I empathize?

It is important that the member receiving the evaluation listen, really listen, to what his or her teammates say without justifying or arguing about what is said. The people receiving the evaluation should just try to meet the communication needs of the team—to understand and to be understood.

4

PROMOTE POSITIVE PROCESSES

A domination of reason would prove to be the
strongest unifying force among men and would
prepare the way for further unifications.
Sigmund Freud

Processes, as used in this chapter, refer to anything that influence the team's progress toward fulfilling its mission and completing its assignments, including elements in the meeting environment and all of the things Think Team members do or don't do in a meeting. Processes are usually quite unplanned and subconsciously caused. They are different than the rules the team is following, the factual content of the problem or the plan it is working on, or the procedure it is following. Processes are considered positive if they help the team and negative if they hinder the team. The purpose of this chapter is to help you become more sensitive to positive and negative team processes, to suggest ways you can promote the positives and avoid the negatives, and to deal with the negatives when they occur.

A Facilitator may be appointed to watch the processes of the team; this person may or may not be a member of the team. In very intense situations or in situations where all members wish to concentrate on the content of the problem or plan, it can help to have an outsider as the Facilitator.

During the training stage of the team's development, the trainer usually serves as Facilitator. The trainer will draw attention to positive and negative processes for the purpose of instruction, but in actual sessions the Facilitator is most concerned with the negative processes. When the Facilitator spots one at work, he or she will stop the work of the team, identify the negative process, and ask the group members how they wish to deal with it. Often, it is only necessary to call attention to the negative process to make it go away. More serious situations will require a facilitation methodology.

The designated Facilitator should try to make himself or herself obsolete because fully trained and developed teams expect every member to accept and discharge the right and obligation to facilitate the team. This means that every member must know how and feel empowered to facilitate as he or she sees the need. The following aids can be helpful:

- **Positive Processes List:** A posted list of positive processes to remind team members what they should strive for during team meetings.
- **Negative Processes List:** A posted list of negative processes to identify the process that is hindering progress.
- **Resolver:** A procedure to help two or more team members systematically resolve a logical disagreement that seems to have stopped the team's progress.
- **Confronter:** A procedure to help team members resolve an interpersonal conflict or a general negative process that is causing sufficient negative feelings in one or more team members and, therefore, inhibiting objective thinking and general progress.

Positive Processes

Positive processes should be encouraged during team meetings to maintain a collaborative spirit and to promote progress. The following list could be posted at each team meeting.

1. Demonstrate commitment to the team's mission, rules, and assignments.

2. Seek objectivity about the assignments and the views of others.

3. Be open-minded, not antagonistic, toward new ideas.

4. Be open and self-disclosing about motivations, feelings, fears, and hopes.

5. Show sensitivity to others' needs and feelings.

6. Seek consensus but be willing to compromise or vote when absolutely necessary.

7. Confront without being offensive; be critical of ideas instead of personalities.

8. Have confidence and be willing to take risks or to go out on a limb without being concerned about how others may view the approach.

9. Use win/win thinking to resolve conflicts by finding ways for all parties to get what they want.

10. Level, be up front and honest, and do not hold back information or opinions.

11. Be friendly and really care for others, but do not attain friendliness and caring at the expense of seeking the truth or the best solutions to problems.

12. Feel no defensiveness or pressure when in the minority position and no sense of righteousness when in the majority position.

13. Show equal respect for all members and ideas.

14. Tolerate and use humor and other tension-relieving activities.

15. Encourage and respect provocative, imaginative thoughts and comments.

Utiliser un lang. propice au respect + a
la bonne entente

Negative Processes

Negative behaviors should be avoided or called attention to when they occur. The following list of negative behaviors could be posted at each team meeting.

1. Violate team rules.
2. Digress—get off the subject.
3. Act uninterested in team's work.
4. Be generally negative.
5. Be overly positive—can't or won't see potential pitfalls.
6. Avoid goal setting.
7. Harbor a hidden agenda or ulterior motive—not let others know what you are really trying to achieve.
8. Assume other individuals are inferior or superior.
9. Contribute to a false unity—unwilling to disagree or go against the majority.
10. Be interpersonally competitive.
11. Refuse to listen to or to try to understand another member; interrupt or "jump" on another member's lines.
12. Be overly concerned with time or deadlines.
13. Misuse power to get one's own way rather than to try to solve the problem.
14. Exhibit defensive and aggressive behaviors.
15. Use manipulative tactics or tricks to influence others.
16. Deliver boring material in a boring way.
17. Misuse humor—sarcasm, ridicule, innuendo. *manipulation*
18. Exhibit prejudice, narrow- or close-mindedness.

→ langage inapproprié (grossier, insultant)

19. Promote an impasse—logic- or emotion-based circular arguments where parties repeatedly state positions with no attempt to resolve differences.

20. Dominate the conversation.

21. Come late or unprepared to meetings or leave early.

22. Be silent, hold back, don't participate in the process.

Team members may have their own "favorite" negative process that they would like team members to take special pains to avoid. If a process is not on the list, add it and then discuss it. Sincere team members should agree to avoid negative processes and be willing to have negative behaviors called to their attention. In most cases pointing out the negative process is all that is necessary to keep things positive.

Resolving Logical Disputes

Logical disputes are those in which the conflicting parties sincerely disagree on some issue or point and do not have any negative or antagonistic feelings toward the other party. Such conflicts can usually be resolved by systematically examining both sides and carefully defining terms. If neither side's position is acceptable to the other, a third way can usually be found to satisfy both parties. Here is a procedure that a Facilitator can use to lead the parties.

1. Agree that one or more logical disagreements exist.

2. Agree that all want a win/win agreement.

3. Identify the issues and write them on a chart page.

4. Agree to deal with one issue at a time.

5. Allow the first person to tell views on the issue with no interruptions, following these steps:

- Report the facts as he or she perceives them;
- Interpret the facts; and
- Suggest a decision.

6. Second person gives feedback on what the first person said to ensure understanding.

7. First person confirms or corrects any misunderstandings.

8. Second person tells views on the issue with no interruptions, following these steps:

   - Report the facts as he or she perceives them;
   - Interpret the facts; and
   - Suggest a decision.

9. First person gives feedback to ensure understanding.

10. Second person confirms or corrects any misunderstandings.

11. Team brainstorms ways to settle the issue, recording the ideas on a flip chart page.

12. Team uses decision-making aids, if necessary, to reach a win/win agreement.

13. Decision is recorded and procedure is repeated for the next issue.

Confronting Negative Processes

Confronting is a form of giving feedback that is excellent for dealing with negative processes because it minimizes bad feelings. It should also be used to let someone know you recognize and appreciate what he or she has done. It is a marvelous way to compliment and encourage positive behavior because it "strokes" without being patronizing. Having team members practice using the techniques with each other on positive processes helps to build a general feeling of goodwill and a bond of trust. It also helps set the precedent for using the technique so that dealing with negative issues seems less threatening.

Either the appointed Facilitator or any team member has the right and obligation to deal with a negative process when he or she feels it is seriously inhibiting the team's progress. Usually, just mentioning the name of the process in a light-hearted fashion is all that is necessary. If the facilitating person believes the casual approach won't be sufficient, he or she should insist that the team stop whatever it is doing. The person asking the team to stop work to deal with a serious negative process should use the following format. Here are the basic steps and an example of how they may be put into practice.

1. Identify the person(s) to whom you wish to address your remarks and get permission to give feedback.

   "Jack, may I give you some feedback?"

2. Describe a conclusion you have arrived at.

   "I get the impression that you really don't want to be here."

3. Tell what you have actually observed that leads you to believe a negative process is at work.

   "I get this impression because you have been constantly looking at your watch and several times you have tried to get the team to come to a decision without fully discussing the problem."

4. Describe how it makes you feel.

   "This is making me very uncomfortable because the problem we are facing is both complex and very important to us all. I'm worried we are going to rush to a premature decision and regret it later. It's making me feel very nervous."

5. Tell what, if anything, you plan to do or what you suggest others do to make all processes positive again.

"I would like to suggest that we either reschedule this session when you can give the issue your full attention or get your agreement to give the problem the attention it deserves now."

6. Invite the other person to give you feedback in a similar format if he or she wishes and reach an agreement on how you plan to resolve this issue.

Notice that in the example given, the Facilitator limited comments to straightforward feedback. There were no put downs, sarcasm, or snide remarks.

Again, members should be encouraged to use this format to give feedback that acknowledges a positive process or promotes positive feelings more often than they use it for negative processes. This will be more appreciated than "attaboys" or general compliments because the receiver will understand what he or she did to deserve the approval. Freely and frequently acknowledging positive processes also tends to boost the spirit of objective cooperation and thereby builds mutual trust and respect among team members.

5

ORGANIZE THE THINK TEAM

*Search all the public parks and you'll never find
a monument to a committee.*
Irvine Page

The quote above correctly reflects the popular attitude toward both committees and meetings in general. Americans often feel ambivalent about functioning as part of a team. Although highly involved in self-development, American office workers get poor marks for blending their talents harmoniously with teammates. This is probably a symptom of the high value placed on individual achievements and on climbing the ladder of success through personal efforts.

A few years ago, the painting of the American signers of the Declaration of Independence was used in an ad with the caption, "It's amazing what the right group can accomplish." Maybe the ad indicates a shift in attitude about groups; but with the exception of team sports and the growing use of work teams in industry, Western culture seems to prefer its models to be singular heroes and heroines. The Japanese, on the other hand, typically do not like to stand out from the group. How can we get the value of both individualistic and group thinking without the negative influences of the two orientations?

Teamwork Thinking is the answer if it is properly used, meaning that it should be used only when results in terms of quality of decisions and wide support are of the utmost importance. Otherwise, let us retain our individualistic values and behaviors because they foster independence, creativity, and respect. Such positive results seem to outweigh the negative excesses of interpersonal competition.

If you have ever participated in a meeting that started with "Let's get right down to business," only to have the meeting end without being the least bit productive, you have paid the price of poor team or meeting organization. Most groups of professionals don't go to work without first making a few basic decisions about how the work will proceed. Professional athletic teams don't, flight crews don't, construction crews don't; however, a group of executives responsible for huge enterprises often think nothing of calling a meeting armed only with an agenda and then proceed to talk in circles for hours with little to show for their efforts at the end of the meeting.

Think Teams, to be worthy of the name, must not only organize themselves at their first meeting, they should also review organizational decisions at the start of subsequent meetings. They do this to make sure everyone still agrees about how they will work together on their various assignments.

True, the team-organization process is simple, even perfunctory for the most part and apparently, to many, trifling. But these are "tremendous trifles" because not attending to them invariably results in wasted time and energy. The following procedure is recommended even for single-purpose teams or for those teams that expect to meet just once. If the team is committed to Teamwork Thinking—to getting the very best thinking from individual team members and to reaching a full consensus decision—the team must become organized.

The detailed team-organization procedure presented will no doubt appear to be excessively detailed for single-purpose teams and to anyone who hates paperwork in general. The procedure presented should be taken as a starting point. Devise your own procedure that will meet the team's needs and, if the team is part of a larger organization, then the organization's needs must also be considered. Keep it as simple as possible to do the job, but be warned against avoiding the organizational process altogether. When a Think Team does not have a common understanding of who it is, why it exists, and how it will operate, it can cause endless hours of unnecessary discussion and poor work results.

Following is a procedure for organizing a Think Team and examples of what might be entered in response to the questions posed by each step.

Step 1. Team Identification

- What is the name of the team?
- What is the name of the organization?
- What is the name of the department or subunit?

Example:

- ABC Team
- XYZ International, Inc.
- Corporate Human Resources Department

Step 2. Mission

- What is the team's purpose for being a team?

A mission is a clear, concise, and complete statement that describes the primary purpose of a team. It is important that the team reach consensus on the exact statement so all members have a common direction and guide for their activities. A team may change its mission statement when it feels the need. The mission statement of the team should not be confused with the mission statement for the entire organization or for a specific assignment. Mission statements are notorious for the amount of time they take to write. This can usually be shortened by starting with a good draft and by recognizing that exactness is not necessary at the start. It can always be modified later.

Example:

To identify and deal with all problems and projects related to the entire engineering department and to make decisions that are within the team's authority. Also, to recommend decisions to management on issues that are important to the team but outside its authority.

Step 3. Team Assignments

- What is the team's assignment?

A team's assignment is derived from the mission statement and describes what the team will work on. Some teams may be formed to handle a single assignment. Therefore, the assignment will be very similar if not identical to the mission statement. Assignments should be understood, accepted, and related to other assignments so all members know their responsibilities and recognize the web of interdependencies that sometimes develops from complex issues. If the team is part of a larger organization, some form of paperwork, such as assignment control sheets, must be used. Progress reports may be required to assure that deadlines are achieved and expectations are met.

Examples:
1. Design a filing system for engineering drawings.
2. Establish a procedure for monthly filing of progress reports in master database, with hard copies sent to all team members and the team's customers.
3. Create database specification criteria and parameters.

4. Submit only final recommendations to the vice president of engineering.

Step 4. Strategies/Policies

- What are the team's strategies and policies for fulfilling its mission?

Strategies are general courses of action upon which specific plans and decisions are made. Policies are guidelines that enable the team to save time when dealing with specific issues.

Examples:

1. We will work on no assignments other than those assigned by management or selected by the entire team. (Strategy)

2. We will meet weekly for two to four hours until the project is completed. (Policy)

Step 5. Rules

- What rules has the team agreed to follow?

Rules are specific requirements the team imposes on itself. The most important rule governing team meetings is how decisions are to be made. Letting the powerful person decide is fine for staff meetings, and democracy is great for reaching politically expedient decisions, but true consensus decision making is superior to either. A consensus decision is not the wimpy, "I can live with what most of you people want" kind of decision; it is the murder-trial-jury type of consensus reaching where everybody must agree before the accused gets the guilty verdict. It takes longer, but sincere consensus seeking forces consideration of majority and minority views and assures full support of the team when a final decision is reached. The team may decide to modify its rules at any time.

Examples:

1. All major decisions must be by full consensus of the team members.

2. Decisions about matters outside the team's authority will be presented as recommendations to those who do have the authority.

3. The next meeting will be planned before the team leaves the present meeting.

4. Members may not send others to represent them at meetings.

5. New members may be admitted to the team on the basis of a consensus decision.

Step 6. Clients/Customers

- To whom will the team deliver the results of its efforts?

The team's customers may be the team members themselves or any individuals or groups that are either external or internal to the organization and who receive the team's outputs. All team members must know exactly who they are working for so efforts can be directed to the customer's requirements. In many cases, there will be a sequence of customers from the one who receives the team's work immediately to the person or group that is the ultimate consumer.

Example:

- Primary Client: Manufacturing Department
- Secondary Client: Zytog Dealers
- Final Customer: End users, purchasers of the Zytog units.

Step 7. Outputs

- What are the products and services that this team will provide to its customers?

Outputs are the products or services that result from the team's efforts. It is important that all team members understand and agree on the principle outputs plus their relative importance and volume. The following example carries through with our engineering department example; other types of teams may only produce a report or, more simply, a decision.

Example:

- Engineering Drawings
- Work Order Specifications
- Feasibility Studies and Reports

Step 8. Members

- Who are the members of the team?

The members of the team are those who plan to meet regularly with the team and share responsibility for the team's work. Keep the membership list current. You may also wish to record "temporary" members or guests.

In addition to the team members' names, it is useful to add such information as titles, organizations, addresses, phone numbers, and areas of expertise for later reference and report distribution.

Example:

Joseph La Cerra, Director Electrical Engineering
Central Engineering
2309 Washington, Building #6
Fremont, California, 56590
(708) 555-6531

Step 9. Reports

- To whom will reports of the team's work be distributed, in addition to the team members themselves?

Reports of the team's work should be given to various members of management, customers, and others who are interested or who may be affected by the team's activities. Include such information as titles, organizations, addresses, and phone numbers.

Example:

So Wan Chi, Vice President, Engineering
(708) 555-6530

Maria Del Rio, Director, Mechanical Engineering
(708) 555-6534
Central Engineering, 32 Bucker Drive
Des Plaines, Illinois 92180

Step 10. Subgroups

- What groups, committees, or other subunits report to the team?

A subunit is one or more persons with a special assignment from the team that is usually done between team meetings. Record any identifying information that may be useful, such as names of members, purpose of each subgroup, and specific assignments for each subgroup.

Example:

- Research Subcommittee:
  (B. Jacobi, L. Brown, N. Ferguson) This subcommittee will handle all research activities to ensure consistent quality.
- Current Assignments:
  ABC Project, XYZ Investigation.

Step 11. Suppliers

- What persons or organizations are customary suppliers to the team?

Suppliers are any persons or organizations that have agreed to meet the team's requirements. In many cases there will be no significant suppliers. In others, they are a vital element of the team's success and must be selected and worked with closely if the team is to fulfill its mission. Enter suppliers' names and all other identifying information that may be useful.

Example:

- Alphabeta Consulting Engineers, Inc.

Step 12. History

- What are the significant events in the team's history?

Significant events in the team's history include anything that the team believes may be useful to record for future reference. Enter succinct statements describing milestones in the team's development or performance.

Example:

- Organized by K. Smith on 2/12 to handle research assignments.
- Team receives formal problem-solving training on 2/23.
- First meeting, Main Conference Room, 3/1.

Step 13. Comments

- What additional comments about the team should be recorded?

Example:

- The office of the president requested that this team be formed.

Step 14. Record Keeping

- Where will the master copy of the team's organization information be kept?
- Who will receive copies and updates?

Example:

- Database #4536-A
- Office of the president
- Vice president for engineering
- All team members

6

MANAGE THINK TEAM MEETINGS

Any meeting worth holding is worth planning.
John J. Kielty

E very meeting must be managed to focus the power of the team on its assignment(s). This chapter offers concepts, tips, and a procedure that can refine your meeting planning and management efforts and thereby increase the quality and productivity of the Think Team.

Consider team sports, which can be an exhilarating or an agonizing experience depending on who you are rooting for. The emotional roller-coaster effect makes it all the more entertaining, which is, after all, the end purpose of play. Win or lose, the world goes on much as before. But look at the team concept in the real world of work or, more specifically, the work of teams in meetings. It could be argued that the real work of teams in organizational life is done between meetings when policies, plans, and decisions are implemented. But let's focus on the meeting process itself. Why? Because, increasingly, the truly important decisions take place in meetings of two or more people and not in the mind of a single leader. Consider war councils, peace conferences, boards of directors, loan committees, project teams, and task forces, to name just a few. The leadership role is important and vital, but even the greatest leader can be more effective if he or she leads independent-thinking, collaborative colleagues instead of followers.

Meetings are still run in a stultifying and formal manner or in a fashion so casual that it's a wonder decisions are made at all. It is possible to use the full creative and critical thinking resources of every member and to get the best possible results both during and after meetings. Here is a ten-step planning and management procedure for meetings in the form of question prompts with example answers. The meeting's Organizer (see Step 3) should complete as much of the plan before the meeting as possible, but his or her work is a first draft that the team can modify at the start of the meeting. A good draft saves considerable meeting time; however, many teams create the plan at the start of the meeting, assuming the members are already organized as a Think Team.

Meeting Planning and Management Procedure

Step 1. Meeting Identification

- What is the name of the meeting?

   Operation Quality Team Meeting
- Meeting date?

   January 17
- Meeting time(s)/Frequency?

   Starting time: 2:00 p.m.

   Adjournment: 4:15 p.m./weekly
- Location of the meeting?

   Conference Room 2

Step 2. Purpose

- Why was this meeting called?

Let people know why you are calling a meeting so they can prepare for it. The meeting purpose may be a general statement such as "Weekly Status Report Meeting" or a specific purpose such as "To decide on the new office location." If several items are to be discussed they could be listed or referred to on a written agenda.

Step 3. Participants and Their Roles

- Who is expected to attend (or is present) at this meeting, and what meeting role have they been assigned?

Enter the names of those members invited and any other identifying information that may be useful later. If you are creating the plan at the start of the meeting, enter who is actually present. Also, name any nonmembers who participate in the meeting.

Identify the roles various individuals have agreed to perform, such as: Organizer, Coordinator, Facilitator, Scribe, Moderator, Member, or Guest. Please note that a person may perform more than one role. Use the following descriptions until the team decides otherwise:

Organizer: The person who has the primary responsibility for planning and calling the meeting. This person should use a meeting plan such as this one. The Organizer usually runs the meeting before and after work has been performed on specific assignments.

Coordinator: The person responsible for arranging the physical details of the meeting such as reserving the room; procuring the equipment, supplies, and refreshments, if necessary; notifying participants; and doing set up. This person is concerned with the room—its lighting, temperature, humidity levels, air flow control—and the arrangement of equipment, chairs, tables, and audiovisual aids. The room arrangement that seems most useful is one table, preferably not too long, with seating on all sides. Square or round tables may be slightly better, but any will do if participants can easily see each other and a screen or monitor.

Facilitator: The team member or nonteam member who watches for negative processes and helps the team deal with them when they interfere with the team's progress. During the team's initial training, the Facilitator serves as a trainer or coach. The Facilitator also provides coaching instruction as necessary during meetings, helps the team evaluate the session, and promotes interpersonal contracts to ensure that future team meetings run smoothly. Ideally, every team member should assume the right and responsibility to help facilitate the team. Even very "mature" teams find it useful, on occasion, to utilize the services of an objective Facilitator.

Scribe: The person responsible for working with the meeting Organizer to complete the meeting report. The Scribe also sees that all flip-chart pages and transparencies that the team wishes to preserve are transcribed and distributed as directed. He or she may also be requested to actually write on the flip charts or transparencies during the meeting under the direction of the Moderator or Organizer. Think Teams have to be precise in their work. This means writing complete thoughts, not just key words, on a chart pad; otherwise, a typist will have to decide what the key words mean later on. The power of the computer is still largely underutilized in team meetings. The computer permits rapid and sophisticated manipulation of the data the team generates. Reports can be immediately printed and distributed. This function may also be performed by the Scribe.

Many will find the team writing process too slow and tedious. Therefore, anything that can be written, either on chart pads or in working papers, before the meeting should be. Members will quickly come to understand the draft concept and the expectation that they are to modify, delete, or replace whatever is written before the meeting. This technique is particularly applicable for mission statements and for assignments where one or more members is in possession of a considerable amount of information that the team will find useful.

Moderator: The person who decides whose turn it is to talk and leads the team through the work procedure selected for a specific assignment. Theoretically, anyone can moderate the team while working on an assignment. While the role may change hands several times during any given meeting, it is usually best to assign the Moderator's role to the person most concerned with the particular assignment. If the team is following consensus rules (full agreement) the Moderator has no more power than any other member to make decisions.

Team Members: Those who are members of a Think Team, whether they also play one or more of the roles described above or not, also have specific responsibilities.

Here are some tips for participating like a professional.

1. *Come prepared.* Gather, study, and think about the problem or issue to be dealt with but keep an open mind regarding how the problem should be solved.

2. *Know your role.* You have been asked to participate because of your experience and your ability to think and work with others. You have not been invited to represent a certain group or a certain viewpoint.

3. *Follow the rules.* The primary rule is that every Think Team member is to be heard and respected; no member is to be considered of higher rank or status while in the session. The goal is to seek consensus decisions. Such decisions require that all members fully agree on all decisions and that voting is to be used only as a last resort.

4. *Understand the process.* The Facilitator/Moderator will help team members to follow systematic procedures, generate ideas, and make decisions. Essentially you will generate lists of items under specific headings. The more aptly and succinctly you can express yourself, the more productive your session will be.

5. *Help facilitate.* Keep interpersonal processes positive and help identify and handle negative processes when you perceive them. Do not hesitate to ask for help or to offer it to others when you see the need for it.

6. *Listen.* Really listen to other team members as you would like them to listen to you.

7. *Enjoy.* To share ideas and reach true consensus on worthwhile issues is one of the highest and most pleasurable forms of human activity.

8. *Have faith.* The right team of problem solvers is a powerful resource.

Step 4. Preparations

- What should be done to prepare for this meeting?

Preparation refers to anything done to make the meeting work. This step should be completed prior to the meeting, but you may wish to record preparations required for the next meeting. Don't forget to assign responsibility for each task. For instance:

1. Distribute reports of last meeting.

2. Prepare chart pages showing agenda and processes.

Step 5. Agenda

- What is the agenda for this meeting?

To build the meeting agenda start with the agenda items and combine like items where possible. Agenda items are anything one or more team members wish to put on the agenda. It is important that all members have their items considered, so write down every suggestion. An item should be described in sufficient detail so that everyone understands what it covers. Identify it as either a "Report Item" or as an "Assignment Item." Report Items are limited to the giving and getting of information and should probably be no longer than ten minutes. Restrict questions to those necessary for clarification. All other agenda items are called Assignment Items and refer to those items that the team actively deals with by following a procedure such as creative problem solving. Next, indicate who suggested the item and the approximate required completion time. For instance:

1. Finance Committee Report—Bill Bailey
   10 minutes

2. Coaxial Cable #34—Assignment/Procedure
   Sara Culver—60 minutes

3. Conference Site Selection—Assignment/Decision
   Alex Gorski—20 minutes

Rank order the items by rating their urgency and importance criteria. This decision technique involves grading each agenda item on a 0 to 10 scale for both urgency and importance and multiplying the two grades to get a rating. Here are two examples:

Agenda Item 1. (Assignment Item)
Importance Grade 9 x Urgency Grade 6 = Rating 54

Agenda Item 2. (Report Item)
Importance Grade 4 x Urgency Grade 8 = Rating 32

The items with the highest ratings should certainly be included in the agenda, although the highest rated item may not be the first one addressed because other factors or policies may come into play. For example, some teams prefer to hear all reports before concentrating on assignments. Plan to cover those items for which you have sufficient time. Write the scheduled time, agenda item, type of item (Report or Assignment), key person responsible (who usually will become the Moderator), time allotted, and the decision rules to be followed.

The exact timing of your agenda may change by mutual consent, but it is important to start with a realistic plan; otherwise, important items may not be given sufficient time. The Organizer should strive to maintain meeting schedule discipline but not too rigidly. The team can decide to alter the agenda by a consensual decision at any time.

Important or interesting topics may come up during a meeting and the temptation to discuss them is powerful. The Facilitator or any member might suggest that the team decide whether to alter the present agenda to deal with the issue now or "capture" the issue and cover it formally at some later meeting.

At times the team may decide not to use a complete procedure because it simply is not necessary. For example, the team may have to make a specific decision such as which of two options must be chosen for an upcoming conference. Or the team may choose to help a member with a nonteam assignment by brainstorming answers to a specific question.

Decision making by consensus is best and is highly recommended for Assignment Items in order to get the best possible work results with the full support of all members. Should there be any reason to make decisions on a specific assignment by the highest-ranking person, as might be the case in a manager's staff meeting, or by voting in order to save time or to meet legal requirements, this should be clearly understood before work begins on the assignment.

Step 6. Results

- What were the decisions or other results for each agenda item?

Record the decisions or results of each agenda item. This step replaces the traditional meeting minutes, which should be avoided unless they are legally required. Assignment Items using a procedure will usually require a separate report. If so, include an explanatory note on the meeting report. For instance:

2:00 p.m.—Finance Committee Report
Bill Bailey
Accepted by majority vote

2:08 p.m.—Coaxial Cable #34
Processing—Sara Culver—60 minutes
Consensus Rules
Completed creative problem-solving procedure steps
    1-4 (see separate report)

3:10 p.m.—Conference Site Selection
Assignment—Alex Gorski
Consensus Decision
Decision made: Omaha Hilton

3:30 p.m.—Plan next meeting
Done

3:40 p.m.—Review Action Items
Done

3:50 p.m.—Evaluate group performance
Done

Step 7. Action Items

- What will the members of the team do as a result of this meeting? By when?

Action items are those things members of the team will do after the meeting. It is important that every member report to the team what he or she will do and when. This feedback activity clarifies communications and enhances commitment to the tasks listed. If there are many assignments, categorize them by the names of the issues or projects or by the names of the members responsible.

Step 8. Next Meeting

- How will the team follow up on action items?

Plan the next meeting before the present one ends. It is important for the team to meet again to follow up on the progress of action items and address any unforeseen issues that may arise. Remind everyone to bring his or her calendar to every meeting.

Example:

- What day and date will the team next meet?
  Monday 7/28

- What are the scheduled starting and ending times?
  2:00-4:00 p.m.

- What is the location?
  Conference Room 2

- What special preparations are necessary? Who is responsible?
  Reserve meeting room—Emil
  Review reports—All members

- What deferred agenda items arose that the group wishes to cover at some later time?

  Conference Catalog ad rates

  Software updates

Step 9. Progress Evaluation

- How successful was the team's work on this meeting's agenda?

This step refers to work on specific Report or Assignment Items. It is important to evaluate and to discuss your progress to improve team performance. Start with a copy of the completed agenda. Evaluate only those items that the group decides to evaluate. You may wish to start by having each member report his or her individual grade of 0 to 10 and offer reasons why the grade was given. Add the individual grades and determine the average or reach consensus for each grade. You may also wish to record summary comments.

Example:

> Coaxial Cable Problem, Grade 7—Team generally feels we got bogged down in unnecessary details that slowed us down and made us lose our perspective.

Step 10. Acknowledgments and Team Performance Evaluation

- With regard to how the group met, thought, communicated, related, and developed as a team, what was good? What could have been better?

This step evaluates the group's performance as a Think Team, not its work on a specific assignment. It is important to evaluate and give members feedback so that positive efforts are acknowledged and areas for improvement noted.

Evaluations can be an elaborate analysis of all meeting elements mentioned in this chapter, or you can simply ask for comments on what was good about the team's performance during the meeting and what could be better. For a more formal evaluation process, use the Team Performance Evaluation at the end of this chapter. Have each team member complete the evaluation individually, then discuss the answers to identify areas in need of improvement.

Example:

> Good: Everyone came prepared.
>
> Could be better: Decision Aids could be utilized more effectively.

To help your team assess its performance, ask the questions on the Team Performance Evaluation below.

Team Performance Evaluation

Grade your team's performance by assigning a number from 1 (low) to 10 (high) next to the following items.

1. To what extent do we seem to know, accept, and deal effectively with our own personal styles of thinking and communicating and with those of our teammates?

2. How well does our team identify and deal with negative processes and counterproductive behaviors during team meetings?

3. How well is our team organized?

4. How well do we tend to plan and manage our team meetings?

5. How well do we tend to communicate factual information during team meetings?

6. How effectively do we generate ideas and encourage creativity?

7. How effectively do we analyze ideas and information and make decisions?

8. How effectively do we select and follow procedures such as creative problem solving?

9. To what extent do we seem to have sufficient background information and facts on our team's assignments?

10. To what extent do we generally seem to meet, think, and work in a quality manner and enjoy doing so?

Scoring Key:

90+ = Host of Angels

80+ = Parliament of Owls

70+ = Flight of Eagles

60+ = Bevy of Quail

50+ = Gaggle of Geese

Less than 50 = Rafter of Turkeys

7

WORK PROCEDURES FOR ASSIGNMENT ITEMS

Socrates: Let us examine the question together, my friend,
and if you contradict anything that I say,
do so, and I shall be persuaded.

Crito - Plato

A work procedure is a series of steps that the team follows when working on an assignment. The steps are best presented as questions because questions are magical prompts to the prepared mind. Obviously the procedure should be appropriate to the assignment; if the team's assignment calls for problem solving, then a problem-solving procedure should be used; if planning, then a planning procedure; if preparing a presentation, then a presentation-development procedure, and so on. This chapter helps you learn how to select and use appropriate work procedures for dealing with Assignment Items.

While the Facilitator, Moderator, or any team member may suggest an assignment work procedure, the team must accept it before continuing and then have the discipline to stick with it and not digress. Use the procedure to guide the team's work. It helps to have the procedure posted where all can see it in order to focus the team's attention on the current step and to give the team a sense of progress.

To select the appropriate assignment procedure, the team should profile the assignment. The following are some items to use to help the team profile an assignment. Again, it helps if the key words are written on a flip-chart page under the heading of "Assignment Profile," for example:

Assignment Profile
Assignment Name: The Lexington Project
Client/Customer: The Bartels Foundation
Assignment Mission or Purpose: Recommend the best way to obtain public support for the Lexington Low-Income Housing Project.
Importance: The Lexington project is the primary project of our most important client and, if successfully handled, will assure our reputation in the industry.
Background Facts: (This section is a numbered list of declarative sentences and supporting data that describes the origins and history of the project to date and how the team got the assignment.)

Review existing procedures such as those in this chapter and Appendix A. They have been used successfully by other teams, but you may modify them or have the team develop its own procedure. The team should follow the sequence of steps in the procedure. One technique is to put each step at the top of a blank chart page and tape the chart pages in sequential order on a wall. Then, should some comment worth capturing come from the team, the Scribe can write it on the appropriate page. Always number each chart page and number each item under each heading.

This system makes for easy reference by any member of the team. The entire process is more or less one of making lists. Clear and large printing, good word choice, and concision and clarity of thought help the process.

The importance of using appropriate procedures with the chart page can hardly be overemphasized. It is the heart of the entire process. It provides the control necessary to link individual team members while providing a vehicle for all thoughts to be recorded. Further, the focus and discipline provided by this approach tend to minimize negative processes.

While it is suggested that the procedural steps be followed as presented, you can go back and forth as new information, ideas, and decisions are developed. At any step in any procedure, the team may also find it worthwhile to use an Idea-Generation or Decision-Making Aid as described in Chapters Nine and Ten respectively.

Following is a list of different work procedures and a recommended use for each. The steps for these procedures and the questions that can guide the team through them are in Appendix A.

1. *Creative Problem Solving:* To achieve a desired end result.

2. *Detective Problem Solving:* To find out what happened.

3. *Scientific Problem Solving:* To discover a principle or law that explains a recurring phenomenon.

4. *Predictive Problem Solving:* To decide what will probably happen.

5. *Corrective Problem Solving:* To reestablish a previous condition.

6. *Planning/Project Management:* To develop and implement a decision or plan.

7. *Presentation Planning:* To develop a persuasive proposal.

8. *Quality/Productivity Improvement:* To ensure the meeting of a client or customer's requirements or to increase production of a product, service, or process.

This chapter contains detailed explanations of two of the most commonly used team thinking procedures—Creative Problem Solving and Planning/Project Management. Chapter Eight is a continuation of the Chapter-Seven topic and is devoted entirely to the frequently used Presentation-Planning procedure. Please keep in mind, however, that there are many other procedures, and the team may design one of its own for any one assignment. As important as selecting and following the right procedure is, it is not as important as having a procedure that the team accepts prior to working on the assignment.

The Creative Problem-Solving Procedure

*The problem fixes the end of thought and
the end controls the process of thinking.*
John Dewey

The Creative Problem-Solving Procedure is the single most useful team assignment procedure because it will work for any type of problem or plan. If you are even unsure about which work procedure to use, it is a fairly safe bet that this one will get you where you want to go. While designed to help solve problems new to the team in new ways, it can also be used to

- Anticipate what is likely to happen;
- Decide what you want to happen;

- Plan to make it happen;
- Prevent things from happening;
- Prevent things from changing;
- Get things back to where they were;
- Keep things going right; and
- Increase production or improve quality.

It is very flexible because any change the team wishes to bring about can be posed in a question about the future; for example, "How can we change condition X to condition Y?" Here are the steps and an explanation of each one.

Step 1. Candidate Facts

- What information should be considered?

Gathering facts is usually the first step in problem solving. However, it is sometimes difficult to judge the relevance of your facts until the team knows what its problem objectives are. Therefore, the team may wish to work on the problem objectives first or work on both the facts (the present situation) and the objectives (the desired situation) at the same time, redrafting and editing until it has a clear picture of where it is now and where it wants to go.

A "fact" is any statement that can be proven to be true. True facts can, then, be logically manipulated to infer new facts. Frequently we confuse opinions and assumptions with facts. In some cases we do not have hard facts to deal with and must resort to using assumptions or probable facts or even loosely held opinions or guesses. However, it is important to recognize when this is the case. It is also important to recognize that few things can be proven to be absolutely true. To compromise with reality, take as facts those statements that can be proven to be true to your satisfaction.

With this in mind, start entering your facts being sure to number each one. You may find it convenient to list "titles" of groups of facts, such as "Current Month Financial Summary," to save time and space. Don't be overly critical of your facts at this time. Evaluation and organization can come later. Be creative in the gathering of facts. Use clear, concise language and include the source of the fact at the end of each entry in case there is a need for clarification later. In some cases the team will find it necessary to delay work until various records and files can be assembled or facts verified. Obviously, it would help to anticipate what information will be needed before beginning work on a problem.

Step 2. Problem Objectives

- What do we want to happen?

Problem objectives are the desired outcomes of the problem-solving activity. It is very important that they be expressed in clear, concise, concrete terms and that they be both realistic and worthwhile. Ideally, they should contain numbers so achievement can be measured. Avoid value terms like "beautify" or "improve." Inexperienced teams tend to set objectives that are too broad and nonspecific. In most cases it will help to set objectives that are based on the facts of the present situation. When these facts are listed, you can then restate them in terms of how the team would like them to read. For example, it might be a fact that a particular department is spending $100,000 per year on supplies. The corresponding objective statement might be "To reduce spending on supplies by $10,000 with no reduction in productivity, which is currently 30,000 units per month."

Here is a sample completed Problem Objectives developed for a manufacturing situation.

Facts: Present Situation	Objectives: 6 Months
Employees = 20	Employees = 15
Production = 200 units	Production = 220 units
Quality = Grade B	Quality = Grade B
Costs = $500.00 per unit	Costs = $500.00 per unit

This objective's statement could also be phrased as follows: "How can we increase the unit production of department X by 10 percent while decreasing the work force by 25 percent within six months without increasing costs per unit or lessening the quality of the product?" However, it helps to use the former method because it is easier to quantify each objective.

Setting objectives is often the most difficult part of problem solving, so most people try to skip over it or do it with little concern for precision. Be as precise as possible, but remember the team can always go back and restate the objectives at any point. Be prepared to modify your objectives at any point in the problem-solving process if new information arises or if your experience indicates that the original objectives were either too narrow or too broad. Take pains to make the objectives clear, concise, measurable, realistic, and worthwhile.

Step 3. Assess Candidate Facts

- What are the relevancy and validity of each candidate fact?

Use the Rater Decision-Making Aid described in Chapter Ten. The basic technique is to have the team reach agreement on each fact by assigning a 0 to 10 weight for both relevancy and validity. Multiply these numbers to get the rating for each candidate fact and then prioritize the facts by putting the one with the highest rating first, the next highest number second, and so on. Those with very low numbers can probably be discarded. Using a numerical approach avoids much circular discussion and facilitates compromise. The entire process tends to clarify thinking and enhance communication and understanding. Expect many facts to be restated as the discussion proceeds.

Step 4. Obstacles

- What's preventing our team from reaching our objectives?

Obstacles are things that the team identifies as hindrances to its problem-solving efforts: what it must get through, under, or around in order to achieve the problem objectives. Listed below are some common categories of obstacles.

- Authority or power
- Communications
- Information
- Money
- Priorities
- Support or opposition
- Technical problems
- Time

The team will have to particularize the categories to its problems. For example, under "Money," the team may identify as an obstacle that the budget allocated for the year has already been spent.

Avoid defeatist or negative thinking. The team is seeking an objective appraisal of the situation and is not looking for reasons why the objectives can't be achieved.

Step 5. Resources

- What does our team have to work with?

Resources are anything the team can use to help it overcome the obstacles and reach its objectives. It is important to know what the team has to work with. Here is a list of the most common resources stated in general categories. The team will have to think of specific resources.

- Data, records, reports, team members
- Equipment, facilities—buildings, etc.
- Materials and supplies
- Money and other financial assets
- Specialists, technicians, professionals
- Team supporters (subordinates, co-workers, leaders, etc.)
- Time

List all resources, even the obvious, and remember the team can always modify the list later.

Step 6. Ideas

- What ideas can we generate to reach our objectives?

The purpose of this step is to generate a large number of ideas on how the team can use its resources to overcome obstacles and reach its objectives. Use the list of resources to find ways to overcome the obstacles identified. Ideas can be generated on approaches, alternative courses of action, causes, effects, options, results, probabilities, or anything else. Note that the purpose is to seek volume, not quality. Judgment is delayed until all ideas have been expressed because critical thinking and evaluation tend to corrupt the creative process. The team will find it helpful to use one of the Idea-Generation Aids described in Chapter Nine. Brainstorming or some variation of it is the most commonly used aid.

Step 7. Edit

- How can the ideas be expressed in terms that describe actions?

Editing means reorganizing and rewriting until there is a cohesive sense to all the ideas the team has generated. This step requires the interplay between creative and critical thinking skills. Most of the ideas generated may be worthless, but the best available decision/solution is probably somewhere on the list. The team will have to critically evaluate each idea and to decide to either accept it as is, cull it because it is useless or covered elsewhere, or combine it with another idea and create a new one.

One or more categories may become apparent when the team reviews all of the ideas it has accepted. It will be easier to work the ideas into a plan if they are rewritten into action terms. This means that each acceptable idea must be stated so that it describes an action that someone will take. Consider the good ideas that are now turned into action statements as the clay from which the team will develop a solution or mold the final plan for reaching its objectives. This may involve putting the ideas into some order such as the sequence in which they will be executed.

Step 8. Decide

- Which ideas will we accept and use?

Some problems require just one major decision, while others will require several minor ones. Major and/or minor decisions may become apparent when editing your ideas. If not, the team will find it helpful to use one or more of the Decision-Making Aids described in Chapter Ten. The types of decisions you will have to make will influence the aid you select.

Step 9. Test

- How will we determine if our decision(s)
  will achieve our objectives?

Some problems have relatively finite solutions. For example, if the problem objective is "How can we determine the reason for the frequent failure of Golper machines?" and the solution is "lubricate all moving parts weekly," the test can be made on a few machines for a few months. On the other hand, many problems have several possible solutions: "How can we reduce teenage pregnancies by 30 percent within three years?" One solution is "a program of sex education." In this example testing will be more difficult. As a matter of fact, determining the right test can be a creative problem in itself. Testing can be done by trying it on a sample situation or by developing a mathematical or physical model to see if it actually works before committing resources to the entire effort. At the very least, it will probably be wise to ask the opinion of experts or those who may be affected by the decision and/or those who have some power to help or hurt its implementation.

An example of testing by trying would be to implement the solution in a single department before implementing it in the entire organization. An example of modeling would be to draw diagrams, to build mock-ups, or to develop computer projections of various "what-if" scenarios. Any major decision to solve a problem or implement a project usually draws both favorable and unfavorable responses from those affected. It would be wise to identify these forces, nurture the positive ones, and minimize the opposition by avoiding deception, ramrodding, and manipulation. If at all possible, convert the opposition.

The final measure of any decision/solution is how well it meets the problem's original or revised objectives. Follow this procedure to test your solution/decision.

1. Review your problem objective(s) and obstacles and judge the likelihood that the decision/solution will overcome the obstacles and reach the objective(s).

2. Ask how the team will test its decision/solution prior to implementation.

In many cases the team's work on the assignment is completed at this point. However, should the solution be one that will take considerable effort to implement, the team will have to carefully plan that implementation. The next section explains how this implementation can be done in a systematic and effective manner.

The Planning/Project Management Procedure

By failing to plan you are planning to fail.
Benjamin Franklin

Planning is a form of problem solving in the sense that the Think Team would like to change a present situation to a desired situation. Once the situations have been determined, the team has to decide on which steps and in which sequence they must be taken to get from one to the other. Also, like problem solving, everyone plans almost intuitively many times a day. When planning is done by a team, however, the intuitive method may not yield the best results because people have different mental habits that are difficult to blend without a conscious and common structure.

The planning procedure offered here, along with the various "subprocedures," is a series of steps the team will find useful to develop and implement moderately complex plans. It should be more than adequate for the kind of planning that most Think Teams do. It is not intended for very complex projects such as those used for engineering projects. Like any procedure, it can and should be modified to fit the team's needs.

The procedure is the Moderator's device for guiding the team as it works on an assignment and should, therefore, be posted on a chart page or displayed where it can easily be seen and referred to as necessary. Title the chart page, number each step, and use key words and/or questions to identify each step.

Here are the major planning steps in both title and question form with subprocedures and explanations.

Step 1. Goals and Objectives

- What generally and specifically should the plan achieve? By when?

To determine goals (general) and objectives (specific) means to identify what will be accomplished and when. The reason for specifying results and deadlines is to give the team a clear target so that resources can be used more efficiently. It is important that the objectives be realistic, measurable, and verifiable so that the team can tell if it has achieved them and can prove the achievement to others.

Determining objectives for a plan is similar to setting objectives for creative problem solving. As a matter of fact, the objectives may be identical; if the team has already completed this step for a problem, it may only need to transfer the decision or solution to this planning step. Remember, the objectives should be expressed in clear, concise, concrete, measurable terms, and they should be realistic and worthwhile.

Following are some questions that will help the team determine the plan's goals and objectives.

1. What are our general goal(s)? Write down whatever a member of the team says. Editing can be done later.

2. What are the key objectives that are expressed or implied in our goal statement that describe something tangible?

3. What unit could best be used to measure each objective?

4. How many of each unit do we want to have when the plan has been fully implemented?

5. By what date and/or time can we realistically expect to accomplish each planned objective?

Here is an example of what might be entered in response to the above questions.

- Goal—To improve the security of the work force by choosing and by installing a new participatory health insurance policy at the lowest possible cost to the employees.

- Objective—By June 30 of this year:

- Obtain proposals from three major insurance companies and select the one that offers the best cost/benefits ratio;

- Design and integrate it into our internal accounting system using less then 100 person-hours; and
- Get 500 or 80 percent of all employees to agree to participate.

Step 2. Tasks

- Who will do what by when?

Following is a five-step subprocedure to help the team answer this question.

1. Identify the major tasks that must be accomplished. The essence of a plan is a description of what the team will do to achieve its goals and objectives. The tasks describe activities—who will do what by when. List anything a team member suggests. Editing can be done afterward. Some examples of tasks are

   - Obtain a list of insurance companies;
   - Poll employees on desired benefits;
   - Determine the difficulty of integration into our system; and
   - Check other companies' experiences with various insurance carriers.

   If many tasks are identified, it may be helpful to put them into meaningful categories such as "Accounting Tasks," "Communication Tasks," and "Selection Tasks" and then relate or prioritize the tasks within each category.

2. Identify the interdependencies of the various tasks.

3. Prioritize related tasks based on their completion sequence or the order in which they must be completed. To relate a set of tasks means to determine

which tasks must be completed before each specific task can be completed. Some tasks are not related to others and may be done at any time. If the tasks in one category are dependent on the tasks in the other categories, it will probably be more efficient to relate or prioritize the entire list of tasks. (See Chapter Ten for more details on how to relate and prioritize items.)

4. Assign deadlines for each task. The timing is usually accomplished by working backward from the deadline for the final task. It will be necessary to have accurate estimates of how long each task or group of tasks will take in order to develop an overall schedule.

5. Assign someone the responsibility for the completion of each task or group of tasks. Rarely will everything go as planned; it just wouldn't be natural. But that doesn't mean the team shouldn't try. Just think what the team will have accomplished if it reaches a consensus decision at this point. Everyone understands and agrees on what will be accomplished and what part he or she will play in the process. This basic agreement is very important. The rest are details, although very important ones, that will be relatively easy to surmount for the dedicated team.

Note that the team may wish to develop two or more sets of tasks to reach the same objectives. In doing so they can compare all plans and select the one that allows the team to reach the objectives in the quickest, most direct or least costly way.

Step 3. Contingency Plans

- What will we do if minimum acceptable results are not obtained at each milestone or checkpoint?

Be ready to change plans if results are not achieved or something beyond your control happens. Here are the steps in the subprocedure.

1. Identify logical milestones or checkpoints when progress will be evaluated. These points can be at the completion of certain major tasks or groups of tasks or at certain specified dates and times, say weekly or monthly.

2. Describe minimum acceptable results at each milestone. This will be easier for those types of plans designed to bring about a steady progression, say from 30 units per week to 50 units per week. In other cases, the plan may be designed to effect some major change upon completion, and interim steps may be more difficult to quantify.

3. Develop contingency plans for each milestone if minimum acceptable results are not achieved. If a certain performance is absolutely required at certain key points, the team must have an alternate plan to which it can switch. Of course, objectives may also be modified to fit reality.

Step 4. Resources

- Which resources in what amounts will be needed to complete each task or group of tasks?

Resources are things needed to complete each of the tasks in the plan. They usually fall into categories such as manpower, money, machines, equipment, supplies, information, experts, etc. Resources needed for a complex undertaking may be difficult to estimate with precision, so the team will have to estimate minimums and maximums. It can then develop totals to estimate the full cost of accomplishing the objectives. The following subprocedure may be helpful.

- Identify the resource categories;
- Estimate the minimum and maximum amount of each resource needed to complete each task in the plan;
- Total each category of resources; and
- Determine when the resources will be needed to complete each task on time.

Step 5. Test/Evaluate

- How will we determine if our plan is likely to be successful?

It would be wise to test and evaluate the plan if it will require considerable time, talent, energy, and resources. This is particularly true if the team must convince others that the plan is worthwhile. The following are examples of ways to do this.

1. Develop cost/benefit figures for each of your plans by identifying the results in each area that will be impacted by the implementation of the plan, then estimate the value of the results in financial or other quantifiable terms.
2. Compare costs/benefits of two or more plans.
3. Get opinions of respected, knowledgeable people.
4. Execute the plan in model form—in mathematical, graphical, or some physical form.
5. Implement the plan in one area, such as in one department or in one geographical location.

Note: Use a Decision-Making Aid, such as the Evaluator described in Chapter Ten, to select the best plan if it is not obvious at this point.

Step 6. Approvals

- Who must approve the plan before we begin? Who should be kept informed of our progress? When and how should reports be made?

This step may or may not be necessary depending on the nature of the team and the relative power of the team members within the larger organization. In some cases formal organizational power may not be a concern, but political power may. It is a good idea if the team considers what persons or groups are likely to be negatively or positively effected by the plan and then takes measures to obtain the support of all concerned.

Step 7. Implementation

- How will we monitor and modify our plan if necessary?

This procedure may or may not be implicit in the original plan. Unlike the Task and Responsibility subprocedures, this step helps you monitor progress and modify the plan when necessary. This will be particularly important if the problem and the solution offered involve considerable risks. Here are the steps in this subprocedure.

1. *Monitor the execution of the plan.* Implementation of decisions or solutions to major problems rarely go as planned. This being the case, monitoring being the case, it is important to devise ways to monitor the progress of the plan and modify it as necessary. This monitoring may be done by checking the completion of the various steps in the plan or by

measuring the intermediate results if practical. For example, the plan may be designed to increase production by ten percent per month for ten months until production has doubled. Thus, the team would watch the monthly production figures to see if the plans are producing the expected results. To use this subprocedure you should identify the following:

- The milestones (checkpoints) when progress will be checked;
- The results that are expected at each milestone;
- The actual results at each milestone; and
- The extent of deviation from the original plan that will be tolerated before the team will reassess the situation and possibly alter the objectives and plans or go to a contingency plan.

This information may be implicit in the plan. If it is not, develop a progress monitoring plan. Such a plan will be particularly important if the problem and the solution involve considerable risks.

2. *Modify the plan when necessary.* Plans must often be modified because of unforeseen events. Planning and replanning is a constant process for any important undertaking. The team may have to change initial objectives, general strategy, a specific step, or the deadlines for achieving any of them. To modify the plans use the following checklist.

- Identify what happened that necessitates a change in the plan;
- Determine if this event will affect the main objectives and the target date/time for achieving them;

- Determine what effect the changes in objectives, if any, or the target date will have on the completion of the tasks and other factors listed in the plan; and
- Develop a new plan if necessary.

Step 8. Results

- How will we measure the final results of our implemented plan?

Whether the objectives have been fully or partially achieved or the team's efforts totally abandoned, it is important to assess the resulting cost/benefits of the work. This assessment can be done more easily and more accurately if the original objectives were stated in financial or other quantitative terms. If not, numbers must be provided for each objective. Here are the steps for this subprocedure.

1. Review the planned outcome of the work found on the Problem or Plan Objectives statement.
2. Describe what actually happened using the same terms as the Objectives statement, if possible.
3. Review the list of resources generated earlier showing the mini/max estimates and enter additional resources categories, if appropriate, and actual figures for each resource used. Determine the total costs for resources used.
4. Total the gains and/or the savings achieved.
5. Compute the net loss or gain.
6. Compute the percentage return on investment.
7. Describe the probable gain or loss of not acting.
8. Write any narrative statements that would help explain the entire effort.

If the entire planning procedure with all its subprocedures seems a "little much" for the kinds of projects in which your team is likely to get involved, remember that the only steps that may be needed are the first two steps: Goal and Objective Setting and Task Identification and Prioritization. Don't use a more elaborate procedure than is necessary, but keep in mind that it is necessary to select and to use some logical procedure to get the best possible results.

8

THE PRESENTATION PLANNING PROCEDURE

Ask, and it shall be given you...
Bible, New Testament

Your Think Team may have a great solution to one of the world's problems and a wonderful plan to implement it, but if it is not accepted by those whose authority or whose support is needed, the effort expended may be wasted. If the approval and/or support of one or more "target" persons is vital to success, a persuasive presentation must be developed and delivered in a way that gives the plan every chance of being understood and accepted. Inexperienced presenters expect target persons to immediately accept a solution or plan simply by hearing about it or seeing it in writing. It doesn't usually work that way. As exciting as the plan is to the team, the target persons have other things on their minds. They have to be convinced the plan will work and will meet their needs. Therefore, the team has the obligation to develop a proposal, present it persuasively, and ask for the needed approval and support.

The presentation procedure offered here is highly detailed and intended primarily for those teams working under the aegis of a structured organization. However, the same basic procedure would apply to situations where the team is trying to convince the general public.

The Presentation Planning Procedure is separated into four phases: Preparation, Presentation, Follow Through, and Evaluation. Following are the step titles and questions that fall under each category, followed by explanations and examples of what might be entered under each. The Think Team can and should answer the questions under the direction of the Moderator while the Scribe records them on chart pages. The work of the team will then normally be refined and put into a written proposal format, and/or an individual or subgroup can be selected and coached to make a live presentation.

Preparation

Step 1. Target

- To whom will the presentation be given? When? Where?

Usually there is one primary target person who must approve the plan before the team can implement it. If so, the team must sell this person—the decision maker—on their plan. However, the team may also wish to present to key persons who will influence the decision maker. The team should ask itself who has the authority to approve the plan. Is someone else's permission needed before approaching the person in authority? Identify the individuals on whom the decision maker depends for decisions like this.

The choice of people to present to is of the utmost importance and must be done with extreme care. Think about the politics of the situation, list candidates, and make the decision systematically, using one of the Decision-Making Aids described in Chapter Ten. Then, get the commitment of the target person(s) to give the plan the time and open-minded attention it deserves. Be prepared to present and/or explain the plan in person and in writing, using whatever props and aids will help the team communicate the plan in a clear, persuasive manner. A professional atmosphere without distractions is important to increase the chances of acceptance.

Example:
> Target Persons: James Jacob, executive vice president, and staff.
> Time: 2 p.m./May 3
> Place: Main Conference Room

Step 2. Presentation Goals

- What do we want our target persons to know, feel, and do when the presentation is over?

Please note that this step is not asking to specify what the plan will accomplish. The overall presentation goal is, of course, to obtain approval of the team's plan, but this step specifically asks the team to identify exactly what it wants the target persons to know, feel, and do. Picture your team leaving the meeting place after the presentation. What do you have now that you didn't at the start of the presentation?

Example:
> James Jacob and staff will:
> - Think the plan is well conceived, tested, and presented.
> - Feel enthusiasm for the plan and respect for the team.
> - Take a committing action such as authorizing the funds to start implementing the plan.

Step 3. Needs

- What are the target person's technical, organizational, personal, and interpersonal needs?

Everyone has needs all the time. The more effectively your plan appears to meet the target person's important needs, the more likely the plan will be accepted. Needs fall into the following categories:

- Technical or work needs, such as quality, price, and delivery time.
- Organization needs, such as obtaining manager or peer approval or adhering to company policy.
- Personal needs, as reflected in general personality traits such as security, approval, fame, acceptance, achievement, challenge, or aesthetic elegance.
- Interpersonal needs in relationship to you, such as respect, dominance, formality, or friendship.

Example:
1. Technical Needs—Finish XYZ project.
2. Organization Needs—Increase profits.
3. Personal Needs—Prestige, respect, status.
4. Interpersonal Needs—With Our Team: To be in control.

Step 4. Aids

- What communication aids will you use to explain, to demonstrate, and to convince the target person(s)?

Aids or props include anything used to help explain, to communicate, to dramatize, and to sell the plan such as graphs, charts, slides, handouts, pictures, models, testimonials, and demonstration materials. They must be well prepared, organized, and handled. Aids will add interest and clarity to the message if chosen carefully and properly used. This takes practice with a live critical audience before the actual presentation. For ideas, consider each step and benefit in the plan as well as the plan's goals. Ask: "What needs help?" "What will help communicate this idea?" Don't overdo it; use only essential items. Remember that the meeting room and everything in it are props in the sense that they can and will influence the presentation. Make sure everything needed is there on time and in working order.

Examples:

- Bar graph of inventory
- Overhead transparency showing key points
- Models
- Testimonials

Step 5. Appointment

- How and when will we set a date to make sure we have the target person's favorable and undivided attention?

Make sure that you obtain the favorable and undivided attention of the target person. It is important that he or she really listen to the plan. Remember that the target person may have other pressing concerns, so take every precaution to make sure the team is respectfully heard. If the plan will be presented only in writing, make sure the target person(s) knows the plan is coming and that the team expects a careful reading by a certain date. If you indicate how the plan will meet the target person's needs, it will help to focus his or her attention. Select a time and place conducive to careful, uninterrupted consideration of the plan.

Example:

Mr. Jacob: Please join the members of our team for a one-hour, private meeting in which we will present a plan to save the organization ten million dollars. We need your approval and support to make it work. Could we meet in the main conference room on Thursday, May 3rd, at 2 p.m.? The members of the team have prepared a formal presentation, and we would like you and your staff's undivided attention for one hour.

Presentation

Step 6. Opener

- What will we say and/or do to open our presentation that will arouse the target person's immediate interest?

Determine who will do the talking and how he or she will open the presentation to arouse immediate interest in the team's plan. The opening is critical because people listen more carefully when a presentation promises to meet one of their important needs. The target person(s) will react most positively to those benefits that meet their needs. It may be a good idea to start with a list of the potential results if the plan is implemented.

Examples:

- This plan will end the concern about mounting deficits.
- This plan is going to make us all look like heroes to the board of directors.
- This plan will save more lives than all the drugs we have developed in the past ten years.

Step 7. Background Information

- What series of facts can we present that will elicit agreement, heighten awareness of the situation, prove we understand the situation, and lead the target person(s) to commit to the need for a solution or plan?

Background facts prove that a need exists for the team's plan. The purpose of presenting them after securing the prospect's attention is to prepare him or her to listen to the presentation with an open mind. This is most effectively done by listing true, pertinent facts that the target persons will readily understand and agree to. The facts should also heighten their awareness of the problem or opportunity, prove you understand the situation, and lead them to commit to the need for a solution.

Example:

1. You said costs have risen steadily this year, right?
2. Management wants a proven way to curb costs, right?
3. You know we helped others with the same problem, right?
4. And now you are ready to look at our plan, right?

Step 8. Plan Name

• What should we call our plan?

Use a brief, catchy name that will sound like the solution to the problem and/or will meet the target person's needs. The name will help him or her to remember and to refer to the plan later.

To pick out a name, list the key words or concepts inherent in the steps and benefits of the plan. Play with the phrases in a creative way until just one seems to fit. One of the Decision-Making Aids described in Chapter Ten will be helpful.

Examples:

• The XK2 Model—The Dollar Saver.
• The Emergency Room Program—The Fire Fighter.
• Product X—The Miracle Maker.

Step 9. Objectives

- How should we describe what our plan will achieve for our target person(s)?

A plan's objectives are what the team expects to achieve when fully implemented. Don't be concerned with repeating earlier statements or saying the same thing in different words but try to be more specific by adding names, dates, and numbers. Consider the target person's needs when selecting and phrasing the plan's objectives.

Example:

> Our plan to introduce the Fire-Fighter Emergency Room Program will cut costs by 30 percent within six months and increase overall profits by ten million dollars by the end of the fiscal year. Listen while I describe how it works.

Step 10. Steps/Benefits

- What are the steps in our plan and how will they meet the target person's needs?

It is important that the presentation is perceived as being fully thought out. Steps are specific actions that will be taken to implement the plan. Use props, aids, and demonstrations to ensure understanding. Give an overview first, then number and name each step, explaining them as necessary.

Benefits are the good things that will result from the implementation of the plan. Explain how acceptance of the plan will meet the target person's needs and solve a problem or realize an opportunity. The benefits should be described in terms the target person(s) will appreciate. Remember target people "buy" benefits—not steps. Don't assume that they understand the benefits—point them out without stressing the obvious or talking down to them. Emphasize those benefits that meet the target person's technical, organizational, personal, and interpersonal needs. Note that in some cases it will be better to point out the benefits of the plan as a whole, rather than for each step.

Example:

- Step One of our plan is to double-check our inventory by the end of the month to make sure that we don't buy unnecessary supplies and run up our cost figures for this quarter.

- Step Two is to ascertain the precise dates we will need each new item so they can be ordered and delivered just in time. Better coordination will save warehouse space and push payouts as far into the future as possible and will also help with our budget problem.

- Step Three is to establish checkpoints and give you reports so that you will never be out of control, etc.

- All these steps add up to the savings of the ten million dollars that we set out to achieve.

Step 11. Costs

- What will the target person(s) have to give in order to get the plan and the benefits it will bring?

Costs are such things as money, time, talent, and other resources that the target person(s) will need to give in order to implement the plan. Be unambiguous and precise. The target person(s) have a right to know what the plan will cost, when it will have to be paid, and how payment will be made.

Example:

This plan will require an outlay of $50,000 within thirty days and twice that figure for the next three months, which will cover costs before savings can be realized. You will also have to assign three professionals and two support technicians full-time to the project, starting within two weeks, in order to meet the schedule we have devised.

Step 12. Handle Objections

- What objections can we anticipate and how should we prepare to deal with them?

Be prepared. Important plans are seldom accepted without concerns being raised. What are they likely to be? How will the team deal with them? Objections or concerns are the doubts that the target persons may have about the plan. They may be real or just things that come to mind and are casually mentioned. Find out before dealing with them by asking. Objections may be avoided by anticipating and dealing with them in the course of the written or verbal presentation. If they come up, the Presenter should have a well-thought-out explanation that shows he or she considered them and has a ready answer for dealing with them.

Before the presentation list every possible objection that may be raised by someone listening to the presentation. Try to prevent the objections from arising by covering the concern in the body of the presentation, but also be prepared to answer each objection. Practice overcoming each objection until the Presenter is confident he or she can deal with each of them effectively.

During the presentation respond to each objection in this way:

a. Verify understanding of the objection by restating the objection. If possible, restate it in the form of a question. Then get an affirmative response from the objector indicating that his or her objection was clearly restated.

b. Answer the objection directly, if possible. If the objection is valid, say so and show how other relevant benefits outweigh the objection. Offer proof if possible.

Example:

Are you saying this cost is too high? (Yes.) Well let me assure you that I have compiled all possible costs, and they are far outweighed by what we get in return. Let me show you the figures.

Step 13. Cause Acceptance

- What small, easy step can we suggest to start the acceptance process?

How will the team's spokesperson ask for approval and make it easy and wise for the target person(s) to say yes to get started? This is the "close" of the selling effort. Don't assume that the plan will sell itself. The target person must be clearly asked to make a positive decision and, if possible, given a reason why he or she should act quickly. Make acceptance easy for the target person. This is important because many people would rather delay than make a decision; they will look for lack of conviction on the team spokesperson's part as an excuse for not giving that acceptance. Be direct without being manipulative.

Ask for commitment and support. They don't come freely, quickly, and easily, have a way to demonstrate the benefits of the plan such as that provided by the Evaluator Decision-Making Aid described in Chapter Ten. Let the numbers sell your plan. Have some phrases prepared that you can use to let your target persons know you are asking for a positive commitment.

Examples:
- If you just say "go," we'll take it from here.
- Just initial this Personnel Release Order and leave the rest to us.
- Choose between these two starting dates and we are on our way.
- If we can get your okay now, we can start the project this week and complete it by the fall. Otherwise, we won't realize the potential savings until next year.

Follow Up

Step 14. Try Again

- How can we prepare the way for a follow-up presentation if our initial efforts are less than completely successful?

Approvals for major projects will rarely be given upon the completion of a presentation, but the team can usually get some feedback about the target person's initial reaction to the plan. Ask for a follow-up date for a decision or for another modified presentation.

Example:

We can see why you can't give us the go-ahead at this point, so when can we set a date for another meeting to deal with your concerns and to get your approval to proceed?

Step 15. Execution

- What will we do to start implementing our plan immediately if we are successful in obtaining approval and support?

The team may be asked what the very first actions will be, should it be given approval. Be ready with an answer.

Evaluation

Step 16. Evaluation

- What was good about our team's presentation and what could have been better?

An evaluation of the team's presentation will require a review of each phase of the presentation plan, including how it was executed and received. This review is important to the team's development because it will help everyone understand why the plan was accepted or rejected. Review the presentation immediately after the presentation; review it again later, after everyone has had a chance to reflect upon the experience. It will prove useful when preparing a future presentation on the same subject or to the same target person(s).

During the presentation review session, use the steps as a guide and ask the team:

- What did we plan to happen?
- What actually happened?
- What was good about it?
- What could we have done better?

Record the answers for future reference. Remember that whether the team was successful or unsuccessful in obtaining the needed approval, it was a winning experience. Everyone learned and grew in the process and became better problem solvers and better able to meet future challenges.

9

IDEA-GENERATION TECHNIQUES TO ENHANCE CREATIVE THINKING

The best ideas are common property.
Lucius Annaeus Seneca

Ideas can be visions of the past, present, or future. Ideas are made up of other ideas and can always be broken down into "idea parts." You can always find a way to break them down into idea parts or find ways to treat them as idea parts and combine them with other ideas or idea parts to generate new ideas.

Creative thinking is the practice of seeing things in nontraditional ways and of envisioning novel possibilities. It is a skill we all have to some extent and one that can be developed through training and practice. Think Teams can be more prolific when it comes to generating ideas not only because there are more minds to tap, but also because the minds stimulate each other. This is synergism in its purest form, and the result is greater than the sum of the parts. Team creative thinking comes into specific play when the team has reached a step in a work procedure where "focused" creativity is called for, that is, whenever the response called for is not obvious and something new may be needed.

While creative thinking is generally important to Teamwork Thinking, the necessity to generate a large number of ideas before making a decision is specifically called for at certain steps in nearly all assignment procedures. Keep in mind that new ideas are often poorly formed and require sculpturing, molding, and refining until they fit the team's needs. Here are some suggestions for thinking creatively.

1. Be as tolerant of your own and your teammates' creative sides as you would be of a playful child because it is from random combinations and undisciplined thinking that new ideas often come.

2. Be patient with those who tend to support traditional values, ideas, and rules to the point of not being able to even entertain novel ideas. They may fear change or just dislike the discomfort it often brings. Be patient—but not satisfied. Show by your own words and behavior that change is not necessarily threatening and certainly can be entertained without hesitation.

3. Encourage team members to ignore boundaries, limits, traditions, precedents, rules, and guidelines when seeking ideas. If you can't ignore them, recognize that they are mostly in your head; you can stretch any of these limitations and get around, under, or through them through in some way or another.

4. Play with things. See things from different angles and in different lights. Combine things or turn them around, upside down, and inside out.

5. Be unconcerned with what others think or what you think they are thinking. Avoid conventional wisdom and behavior. Be less inhibited by artificial restrictions on your thoughts.

6. Separate critical thinking from creative thinking. While they overlap and both are needed to solve problems, it often helps the flow of creative ideas if we turn off criticism and control. Suspend judgment while creating.

7. Be tolerant of yourself and others when treating serious things playfully. Playfulness may seem insensitive but it can be a tension reliever. More importantly, it can be an attempt to approach a problem creatively.

8. Avoid squelching reactions to new ideas by comments such as the following:

That won't work in this organization.
We tried that last year.
That will cost too much.
The boss would never go for that approach.

Idea-Generating Techniques for Think Teams

There is no way to decide which of the Idea-Generation Techniques described below will be most helpful for the problem you are working on. Any one or all of them may be used successfully. They all have one thing in common— they are most effective when critical attitudes are suppressed. Their purpose is only to "generate" ideas, not necessarily "good ideas." Just believe that if the team can generate a sufficient number of ideas, it is more likely to generate one it can use. Here are some ways each team member can generate ideas.

Mental Delegation. Tell your subconscious to find solutions for you, then "sleep on it" or let it "perk on the back burner" until an answer pops into your head.

Mental Projection. Try to get inside things, even inanimate objects, and think about how you would feel and how you would see things from these new perspectives. Or imagine yourself in target situations and note what you see and feel.

Modeling. Use pictures, mock-ups, graphs, representations, analogies, or numbers to escape the confinement that words may impose on the expression of some ideas.

Spontaneous Generation. Answer a spoken or unspoken question. You do it every day subconsciously. For instance, you may be tired and wish to rest. This is your problem. You ask yourself, "How can I sit comfortably?" and, thereby, generate the idea "sit in a chair."

Idea Analysis. Break down a main idea into its constituent idea parts. For example, the idea parts of a chair could be color, material, design, legs, sitting surface, back, fasteners, glue, etc.

Idea Synthesis. Add your main idea to other related main ideas. Combine chair with table, lamp, and cabinets and generate the embracing main idea "matching furniture."

Analogizing. Look for the similarities in your problem to things that already exist. For example, think of support columns as tree trunks or imagine how gears mesh to explain the intermixing of groups of people. This searching for analogies may lead to fresh ideas.

Alternate Viewing. This is simply the process of looking at something from different perspectives for purposes of finding new uses or explanations or simply understanding it. Look at it upside down, inside out, backwards, forwards, and consider it from every conceivable angle and from every possible perspective.

Hypothesizing. This is the act of playing "What if?" What if we made it big as a house? What if everybody wanted the same item? What if we found a million dollars? etc. Imagining one variable change can lead to ideas about other changes that can be useful.

Forced Relationships. This is the process of systematically combining things that normally are not considered ones that go together to see if you can develop a new idea. You may combine products like grease with a salt shaker or combine parts of a thing with the parts of another thing just to see what you can create.

Attribute Listing. This process takes an item and systematically lists all of its parts and functions to get a fresh perspective on the item. This process can, then, lead to ideas about adding or subtracting attributes to see what new item can be developed.

Four Idea-Generation Aids have proven to be of particular use for Think Teams: Brainstorming, Checklist Questioning, Category Combining, and Scenario Development.

Brainstorming

The purpose of brainstorming is to help the team generate a large number of ideas. It is most often used when the team reaches the Generate Ideas step in the Creative Problem Solving procedure, that is, "How can we use our resources to overcome our obstacles and reach our objectives?" The team can also use brainstorming alone to develop ideas for new approaches, alternative courses of action, possible causes, special effects, new options, ideal results, other probabilities, or anything else it wishes. Then it can mix and match the ideas and continue the process almost indefinitely. Please note that the purpose of brainstorming is to seek volume, not quality. All team members should avoid judging until all ideas have been expressed because critical thinking and evaluating tend to corrupt the creative process. The following are some suggestions for brainstorming.

1. Make sure all team members understand the primary brainstorming concept, which is the challenge to generate as many ideas as possible. They should also be informed of the brainstorming meeting format and rules.

2. If practical, team members should be told what question will be brainstormed before the meeting, or they should be allowed time in the meeting to do some individual brainstorming before the team brainstorming session begins.

3. Use a meeting room where chart pages can be taped to the walls. Write the question to be brainstormed on the first page of the chart. The Scribe records on the chart pages whatever a team member offers and numbers it; the scribe then tapes each written idea from left to right across a wall.

4. The process starts by a team member taking a turn telling one of his or her ideas.

5. At any time, team members may shout out ideas sparked by those being read. They don't have to wait their turn if the idea is new to them at that moment. This process is called "tailgating."

6. The social atmosphere should be permissive. Anything goes—playfulness and random thoughts are encouraged. All ideas are recorded, regardless of how silly or impractical they may seem, because they may stimulate other good ideas.

7. Negative remarks, actions, and attitudes are absolutely forbidden. Violators should be curbed immediately in a good-natured manner.

8. After many ideas are recorded, try to think of ways two or more may be combined to form new ideas.

9. Don't be limited to words. Play with models and drawings of any kind to change perspectives.

10. Use analogies, similes, and metaphors to describe ideas.

11. Team members should try to relax and enjoy themselves. Team creating is one of the highest forms of human mental activity.

12. When the well of ideas seems to have run dry, it is a good time to take a break or even to end the meeting. This will also help to make a clean break between the creative and critical modes of thought.

13. Team members can continue to think of more ideas before the next session. Do this by frequently reviewing a typed copy of all brainstormed ideas between sessions to help stimulate more ideas.

Checklist Questioning

As mentioned earlier, questions work as prompts to the prepared mind. They help team members leap from the known to the possible. This technique involves the use of the same question "stem" with several possible endings as shown in these examples.

1. How can our product be made less expensive? More durable? More attractive?

2. How will our proposal be received by management? Labor? Government regulators?

3. What will the effect be on our economy if interest rates decrease? Oil becomes unavailable? Emigration increases?

4. What reaction to this event could we expect from the Chinese? Japanese? Australians?

5. How would this new design concept be applied to bathrooms? Kitchens? Recreation rooms?

6. What would happen to sales if we increased prices 5 percent? 10 percent? 15 percent?

Use a separate chart page for each possible answer. Invite members to write their ideas under each heading or shout them out and have the Scribe record them. Write down every idea answer you can think of before editing the list. Answers that seem silly at first may trigger other ideas that do have value. Remember, the point is to generate many ideas and not just good ideas.

Here is a list of common factors that you could use in a checklist with or without a question stem.

- Who, what, why, where, when, how
- Add, subtract, multiply, divide
- Past, present, future
- Months of the year
- Days of the week
- Seasons
- Alphabet
- Parts of the human body
- Compass points
- Clothing items
- Rooms in a home
- Times of the day
- Parts of the world
- States of matter (solid, gas, liquid)
- Temperature ranges
- Tastes or smells

- Money, manpower, machines
- Climates or terrain
- Body positions
- Moods or feelings

Category Combining

Category Combining is the procedure of matching an item in one category with items in one or more other categories.

1. Identify the category headings.
2. List the items in each category.
3. Write out all possible combinations or select the best combinations.
4. Prioritize the candidate combinations to select the one(s) to be used.

For example, if you would like to generate ideas for writing a story, you might list the major categories as: "Male Lead," "Female Lead," and "Conflict." Under each of these, you would list all the variations you could think of. For example, under Male Lead you might list warrior, politician, and jewel thief. Under Female Lead you might list doctor, mother, heiress. Under Conflict you may list the male lead's terminal illness, the two leads' conflicting political loyalties, or a blood feud between their respective families. When you are finished listing the categories and options, you can pick out various combinations or reconstruct the list to show all the possible combinations in the following format.

Male Lead	Female Lead	Conflict
Warrior	Doctor	Terminal Illness
Warrior	Doctor	Political Conflict
Warrior	Doctor	Blood Feud

| Politician | Doctor | Terminal Illness |
| Politician | Doctor | Political Conflict |

....and so on.

Scenario Development

To develop a scenario means to spin a yarn or to write an imaginary, yet realistic story line based on known facts, assumptions, and probabilities. It is sometimes helpful to develop several scenarios based on the same facts but with different attitudes, such as best case, worst case, or most likely case. This technique can be used to explain what happened in the past, to develop a hypothesis when scientific problem solving, or to anticipate future events.

1. Title the scenario.
2. Identify the tone (e.g., optimistic, pessimistic, realistic).
3. Set the time period (past, present, future).
4. Locate the setting—where does the story take place?
5. Cast the story—who plays what roles?
6. List the props—what nonhuman elements are important?
7. List the events that take place in sequential order.

While scenarios can be developed to explain past events, such as how a crime was committed, they are most often used to speculate what the future will be like if certain team decisions are made. Then the team can use one of the Decision-Making Aids described in Chapter Ten to reach a consensus on which scenario is most likely to happen and to prepare contingency plans.

There are no doubt many other Idea-Generation Techniques the team could successfully employ. The important things to remember are that everyone has a creative capacity, teams can generate more ideas than individuals, idea generation is a vital Teamwork Thinking activity, and all ideas are the product of the team and not of individual members.

10

DECISON-MAKING AIDS
TO ENHANCE
CRITICAL THINKING

*A vote recorded by 40 academicians is not better
than a vote of 40 water carriers.*
Gustave Le Bon

*The most successful decision makers follow
a set of rules that helps them select the best
alternatives under the circumstances.*
Philip Branstetter

Decision-Making Aids help Think Teams to systematically manipulate information to arrive at a consensus decision. They are used at any step in an Assignment Procedure that calls for a decision, especially when making the decision is not obvious or easy. They can also be used alone, outside of the context of a procedure, to make one or more decisions.

Decision making is the overt expression of critical thinking which is more commonly defined as "the practice of examining statements or expressions and determining their validity and usefulness." It is a skill we all possess to some degree and one that can be refined through training, practice, and the desire to improve. Critical thinking is an important skill for Teamwork Thinking because decisions depend on the evaluation and manipulation of facts, the use of logic to develop and test ideas, and the making of many quick and systematic discriminations. Teams can be more critical in their thinking than individuals because of the different aspects and insights that individual group members are likely to have. While every member of the team should generally strive to think critically, except when specifically engaged in creative thinking, critical thinking is of special importance when the team is at a step in a work procedure that calls for overt decision making.

Here are some suggestions to enhance your individual critical thinking ability.

1. *Information based on your own direct perceptions is usually more reliable than other sources.* However, your perceptions may be wrong due to your own preconceived ideas or prejudices. Things may not be what they seem, so keep an open mind and try to see things from the viewpoint of those who disagree with you.

2. *Be careful about your assumptions.* You may have adopted them when you were less astute in your observations but continue to use them, despite the availability of new evidence. You may use them so automatically that you are not aware they have slipped into your reasoning processes. "We can't let Mavis handle this assignment, she's just a kid."

3. *Test assumptions whenever possible.* Facts can only be deduced from facts. If your premise is wrong, your conclusions are likely to be wrong. "No family in this township is impoverished; we don't need a welfare program."

4. *Avoid generalizations, particularly hasty ones or those based on too few observations or facts.* "There is no serious unemployment problem, just look at all the job ads in the daily paper."

5. *Be sensitive to the difference between facts and opinions.* Facts can be proven: the best ones repeatedly. Opinions, regardless of how strongly held and sincerely expressed, cannot be relied on. "I'll stake my reputation and my next paycheck on this information; this source has been one hundred percent reliable in the past."

6. *Logic may be the best tool we have for inferring the truth from facts.* Unfortunately, using logic can often lead to

error because some words have more than one meaning and will be interpreted differently by various team members.

7. **Don't jump to conclusions.** Get all the pertinent facts first; if the facts are insufficient, go get more facts before making a decision. "The boss didn't object when I suggested we leave early, so it must be okay with her."

8. **Tend to suspect precedents, rules, generalizations, or dictums that seem to have the truth all wrapped up in a neat little package.** They may be true, but they are often used as a springboard to nonsense. "People come into the world with no hates or prejudices, so we need only tap into their basic good instincts and trust them to do the right thing."

9. **Use quantifiable terms whenever possible because numbers can be more accurately and more easily manipulated than words.** However, numbers can also be used to confuse and obfuscate. Remember the warning about there being three major types of lies: lies, damn lies, and statistics. Or "Some people use statistics like a drunk uses a light pole, more for support than illumination" and "You can drown in a stream with an average depth of one foot."

10. **Beware of analogies, similes, and metaphors.** They cannot prove; they can only illustrate someone's opinion. "He's as innocent as a new born babe."

11. **Watch for illogical leaps.** An example of this is a statement such as "The most terrible wars in history have occurred since women gained the right to vote." The events are not connected, even though one preceded the other.

12. **Consider the source of the information.** The source person may consciously or subconsciously present opinions as though they were facts or have his or her objectivity clouded by his or her own system of values. "He wouldn't lie, he belongs to my church."

13. *Question everything to uncover and validate facts.* Facts are essential to understand a problem, to evaluate proposed solutions, and to test results.

14. *Strongly held values and beliefs can alter perceptions and inhibit objective analysis and synthesis of facts.* "The captain just wouldn't make a mistake like that, he's a West Point graduate."

15. *Break big problems into smaller, more manageable ones and solve the parts until the entire problem is solved.*

These suggestions for individual critical thinking should be incorporated into the following team decision-making techniques.

- **Prioritizing:** To rank order several items.
- **Grading:** To assign a grade to several items.
- **Rating:** To rate items on the basis of two interdependent variables.
- **Evaluating:** To evaluate one or more items using two or more weighted criteria.

Prioritizing

Prioritizing is one of the most useful and powerful decision-making techniques for Teamwork Thinking. Many, if not most, problems or important parts of problems require the team to determine the rank order of a number of items according to one or more criteria. It is particularly useful when all options or alternative items must be considered in relation to all others, such as when you must decide on several actions and determine the order in which they should be taken to achieve your objective most efficiently. Other criteria may also be used such as importance, urgency, cost, ease, value, and so on. The choice may also be a composite of several factors or simply the best or most preferred of the two being considered. In effect, the entire decision is made up of a number of lesser decisions. Here is how a team can systematically prioritize a list of items. (The process is also shown in Figure 1.)

1. List the items to be prioritized both vertically and horizontally on a grid and assign a letter to each item so that you have A,B,C, etc., across the top and down the side, making sure the same letters are used for the same items. Put a plus sign in the squares that represent the same letter on the top and side.

2. Work down the horizontal list. Start with "A" and compare it to each item in the vertical list. If "A" is more important or should come first according to some other criteria, put a plus (+) in the appropriate square. If it is less important or should come after the item in the vertical list, put a minus (-) in the appropriate square.

3. Total the plus marks vertically. Note that a plus has already been entered where identical letters meet, so no column totals zero.

4. The lower the number, the higher the priority. The lettered item with a total of one would be first, the letter with two would be second, and so on.

Figure 1 is an example of how the Prioritizing Aid could be applied to determining the order of tasks required to make a sandwich.

Prioritizing Aid							
	A	B	C	D	E	F	G
A Serve sandwich	+	+	-	-	-	-	-
B Clean up table	-	+	-	-	-	-	-
C Put on plate	+	+	+	-	-	-	-
D Toast bread	+	+	+	+	+	+	-
E Cook eggs	+	+	+	-	+	+	-
F Build sandwich	+	+	+	-	-	+	-
G Buy eggs	+	+	+	+	+	+	+
Total Rank	6	7	5	2	3	4	1

Figure 1. Prioritizing Aid

Grading

Grading is the process of assigning a 0 (low) to 10 (high) value to a number of items. The number represents the extent of one or more qualities. Grading can also be done for two or more criteria. Combining, totaling, and averaging the grades can be more useful than prioritizing in some situations because it allows for greater shading of opinions and ties. The grading procedure is as follows:

1. List the items;
2. Identify the qualities important to the decision;
3. Grade the qualities on a 0 (low) to 10 (high) scale for each item;
4. Total and/or average the grade for each item; and

5. Rank order them according to their totals or averages.

Figure 2 is an illustrated example of the Grading Aid used to select a new hire from several job candidates. The qualities are

A = Experience
B = Education
C = Availability
D = Cost to Relocate

Item No.	Items	Qualities				Total	Avg.	Rank
		A	B	C	D			
1.	Ellen O.	6	7	4	3	20	5	3
2.	Mike S.	5	7	9	4	25	6.25	1
3.	John L.	8	2	4	8	22	4.5	4
4.	Lill K.	5	5	5	9	24	6	2
5.	Ron N.	2	2	4	4	12	3	5
	Totals	26	23	26	28			
	Averages	5.2	4.6	5.2	5.6			

Grading Aid

Figure 2. Grading Aid

Rating

This technique is especially useful for applying two equally powerful and interdependent criteria to various options. The Rating procedure is as follows:

1. List the items to be rated;
2. Identify criteria A and B;
3. Grade each item 0 to 10 (high) for each criterion;
4. Multiply grades to get rating; and
5. Rank order by making the highest rating first.

Figure 3 is an example of this technique used by a Think Team of urban planners who, when using the Creative Problem-Solving Procedure, had to rate the candidate facts they assembled. Criteria A = Validity and B = Relevancy.

No.	Items	Extent of Criterion A x	Extent of Criterion B =	Rating	Rank
		(Validity)	(Relevancy)		
1.	30 miles to New York	10	3	30	4
2.	72,000 students	10	8	80	2
3.	60% Blue collar	7	8	56	3
4.	300,000 families	9	10	90	1
5.	20% Hispanic	9	1	9	5

Rating Aid (table title)

Figure 3. Rating Aid

Evaluating

Evaluating is the most powerful Decision-Making Aid because it can be used with any number of options and criteria. It appears quite complicated but can be quickly learned with a little practice. Here are the instructions followed by an example using the Evaluator Decision-Making Aid (Figure 4). (Note that each step is agreed upon by the entire team. For those that require a number, the average of the team members' views may be used but only if full consensus seems impossible to achieve.)

1. Select options.
2. Select criteria.
3. Weight each criterion by assigning a + or - value depending on whether much of it is good or bad and a 0 (low) to 10 (high) to indicate the extent that it is important to the decision.
4. Decide on the extent of positive correlation of each option to each criteria, using a 0 (low) to 10 (high) scale.
5. Multiply each criterion weight by the extent of positive correlation. The highest number indicates the best option.

Example:

When should we start the Quagmire Project?

Option 1. Summer

Option 2. Winter

Criteria and their weights:

a. Comfortable working weather (+ 8)

b. Availability of personnel (+ 6)

c. Cost (-7)

Extent of positive correlation between options and weighted criterion:

Of option 1 to Criteria A is 9   (9 x +8 = 72)

Of option 1 to Criteria B is 5   (5 x +6 = 30)

Of option 1 to Criteria C is 4   (4 x -7 = -28)

                                     Total +74

Of option 2 to Criteria A is 3   (3 x +8 = 24)

Of option 2 to Criteria B is 9   (9 x +6 = 54)

Of option 2 to Criteria C is 6   (6 x -7 = -42)

                                       Total +36

Decision: Option 1. Start in the summer.

Evaluator Decision-Making Aid							
		Options					
		1. Summer			2. Winter		
Criteria	Weight	Corr.		Answ.	Corr.		Answ.
A. Weather	+8	x	9	= 72	x	3	= 24
B. Personnel	+6	x	5	= 30	x	9	= 54
C. Cost	-7	x	4	= -28	x	6	= -42
Totals				74			36
				(Decision)			

Figure 4. Evaluator Decision-Making Aid

APPENDIX A:
EIGHT WORK PROCEDURES

Following is a list of different work procedures and a recommended use for each. To follow any work procedure, answer the questions following each heading.

1. **Creative Problem Solving:** To achieve a desired result.

2. **Detective Problem Solving:** To find out what happened.

3. **Scientific Problem Solving:** To discover a principle or law that explains a recurring phenomenon.

4. **Predictive Problem Solving:** To decide what will probably happen.

5. **Corrective Problem Solving:** To reestablish a previous condition.

6. **Planning/Project Management:** To develop and implement a decision or plan.

7. **Presentation Planning:** To develop a persuasive proposal.

8. **Quality Productivity Improvement:** To ensure the meeting of a client or customer's requirements to increase production of a product, service, or process.

Creative Problem Solving

Purpose: To achieve a desired result.

1. Candidate Facts: What information should be considered?

2. Objectives: What do we want to happen?

3. Assess Candidate Facts: What is the relevancy and validity of each candidate fact?

4. Obstacles: What is preventing our team from reaching its objectives?

5. Resources: What does our team have to work with?

6. Ideas: What ideas can we generate to reach our objectives? (Use the list of resources to find ways to overcome the obstacles identified.)

7. Edit: How can the ideas be expressed in terms that describe actions?

8. Decide: Which ideas will we accept and use?

9. Test: How will we determine if our decision(s) will achieve our objectives?

Detective Problem Solving

Purpose: To find out what happened.

1. Event: What happened that you don't understand?

2. Candidate Facts: What information should be considered?

3. Organize Facts: How can we organize the facts so that they can "suggest" ideas and additional facts?

4. Theories: What theories could explain the facts?

5. Evaluate Theories: What theory best explains the facts and the event?

6. Test: How can the theory be tested?

Scientific Problem Solving

Purpose: To discover a principle or law that explains a recurring phenomenon.

1. Background Facts: What information should be considered?

2. Phenomenon: What is the key question to be answered?

3. Hypothesis: What theory explains the recurring phenomenon?

4. Experiment: What test or experiment will prove or disprove the hypothesis?
5. Data: What data did the experiment(s) yield?
6. Results: How was the original hypothesis proved or disproved?
7. Law: What principle, rule, law, or other conclusion can you draw from the data?
8. Follow-Up: What further tests and experiments should be made?

Predictive Problem Solving

Purpose: To decide what will probably happen.

1. Present Situation: What is happening now?
2. Past Situation: What has been happening?
3. Normal Trends: Based on the past and present situations what is the trend for the future?
4. Influencing Circumstances: What events are likely to take place that will influence the normal trend?
5. Future Situation: Based on projections of normal trends and the likelihood of various external factors, what are the possibilities for future situations?
6. Predictions: What is likely to happen at various points in the future?
7. Actions: What, if anything, should be done as a result of current predictions?

Corrective Problem Solving

Purpose: To reestablish a previous condition.

1. Desired Situation: What should be the present situation?
2. Actual Situation: What is the present situation?

3. Events: What happened that may have influenced the present situation?

4. Organize Events: How do the events relate to each other in terms of cause and effect and/or in a time sequence?

5. Correction Points: What must be changed to alter results in the desired way?

6. Plan: Who will do what and by when to make the necessary corrections?

Planning/Project Management Procedure

Purpose: To develop and implement a decision or plan.

1. Goals and Objectives: What generally and specifically should the plan achieve? By when?

2. Tasks: Who will do what? By when?

3. Contingency Plans: What will we do if minimum acceptable results are not obtained at each milestone or checkpoint?

4. Resources: What resources, in what amounts, will be needed to complete each task or group of tasks?

5. Test/Evaluate: How will we determine if our plan is likely to be successful?

6. Approvals: Who must approve the plan before we begin? Who should be kept informed of our progress? When and how should reports be made?

7. Implementation: How will we monitor and modify our plan if necessary?

8. Results: How will we measure the final results of our implemented plan?

Presentation Planning/Management Procedure

Purpose: To develop a persuasive proposal.

1. Target: To whom will the presentation be given? When? Where?

2. Presentation Goals: What do we want the target person to know, feel, and do when the presentation is over?

3. Needs: What are the target person's technical, organizational, personal, and interpersonal needs?

4. Aids: What communication aids will we use to explain, demonstrate, and convince the target person?

5. Appointment: How and when will we set a date to make sure we have the target person's favorable and undivided attention?

6. Opener: What will we say and/or do to open our presentation that will arouse the target person's immediate interest?

7. Background Information: What series of facts can we present that will elicit agreement, heighten awareness of the situation, prove we understand the situation, and lead the target person to commit to the need for a solution or plan?

8. Plan Name: What should we call our plan?

9. Objectives: How should we describe what our plan will achieve for our target person?

10. Steps/Benefits: What are the steps in our plan and how will they meet the target person's needs?

11. Costs: What will the target person have to give in order to get the plan and the benefits it will bring?

12. Handle Objections: What objections can we anticipate and how should we prepare to deal with them?

13. Cause Acceptance: What small, easy step can we suggest to start the acceptance process?

14. Try Again: How can we prepare the way for a follow-up presentation if our initial efforts are less than completely successful?

15. Execution: What will we do to start implementing our plan immediately if we are successful in obtaining approval and support?

16. Evaluation: What was good about our team's presentation and what could have been better?

Quality/Productivity Improvement Procedure

Purpose: To ensure the meeting of a client or customer's requirements or to increase production of a product, service, or process.

1. Process Improvement Opportunity: What is the area or activity that might be improved?

2. Customers: Who are the customers for the team's outputs?

3. Customer Requirement: What does the customer need, want, and expect from the team?

4. Supplier Specifications: How do the customer's requirements translate into our work specifications?

5. Work Process Steps: What steps, tasks, and/or activities must be performed to do the specified work?

6. Critical Measurements: What information will you collect to measure the quality of the output of the

work process? How and where will it be collected? (Preferably this will be at the source of the activity.)

7. Process Evaluation: How will we determine if the work process produces an output that consistently meets the process specifications and satisfies our customers?

Optional Steps

8. Results Evaluation: What happened? Is the customer satisfied?

9. What's Next? What can we do to further improve quality and/or productivity?

INDEX